Introduction

First you must be willing to humble yourself enough to admit your faults and strong enough to do something about them. LA4 is designed to help you in this process. All you have to do is be willing to change and say, "I will."

Why LA4? LA stands for Life Applications and the 4 represents the four areas of focus:

- [ ] Developing Practical Living Skills
- [ ] Building Strength of Character
- [ ] Clearing the Clutter
- [ ] Establishing Hope and Vision

Are you courageous enough to put it in writing? Maybe you're curious enough to commit yourself to the following: "I'm willing to change. I'm willing to get out of the puddle of boredom and wasted time and embark on a life-changing experience that can only lead to success, prosperity and fulfillment." –LA4.

All right! Let's get to work on your future.

Troy
_____
Troy Kidder - Author

_____
Your Signature

LIFE APPLICATION 1

Developing Practical Living Skills – **SECTION 1**

LESSON 1

> **LA4 TERM** Honoring relates first to those people who are in authority over you—namely your boss.

The idea is to make them look good, to build them up. It means treating them with respect. The first and most powerful way to honor authority figures in your life is to not only do what you're told, but do it without grumbling or complaining. (Let's face it: we don't like it when other people whine.) It means doing your best for them even when they're not around or even when, in your opinion, they may not deserve it.

We also should honor our fellow human beings: our friends and neighbors. We do this by considering their needs above our own, by treating them the way we like to be treated. This takes a little extra effort on our part. We must be alert to others' situations and needs—for example, doing an extra job for someone who cannot repay, or maybe sending someone a note of encouragement. It's little things that can make a big difference in someone's day or even in his or her life.

Honoring others will make you a person of honor.

Quick thought

Think about it. If you begin to honor those around you, what boss wouldn't want to see you prosper? What boss wouldn't promote you … giving you more responsibilities and even privileges? Who wouldn't want to be your friend when your desire is to see them prosper first? This is a powerful concept that will change your life if you choose to practice it. I guarantee it!

But this is not a short-term goal. If you begin to honor others even more, it may take a while, but ultimately you will prosper even more because of it. In some cases you may receive instant positive reactions to your actions, but in many cases you won't, and that's OK. This is a lifestyle. It's day-in and day-out. Be content with a job well-done. We treat others with honor because it's the right thing to do, not because of the response we get from them or not for what it will do for us. However, if you begin living this way, don't be surprised if people start going out of their way to honor you. And more importantly, you will make a positive impact wherever you go.

Why? Because very few people live this way. You can. It's a choice.

LA4 - To Honor

Journal entry

What are some things you can start doing now that will help you improve the way you honor those in your life? Also, looking ahead, can you already guess (if you begin to live this way) how it will change your life and the lives of those around you?

Discussion questions

Discuss the journal topic. Borrow ideas from each other.

_____
_____
_____
_____
_____
_____
_____
_____
_____
_____
_____
_____
_____

Life applications

Begin to practice these ideas of honoring at a deeper level. Notice how people respond differently to you, and remember, the real change will be long-term.

© 2000 - 22 TROY... Pure Blue Creative, LLC LA4™

Developing Practical Living Skills – SECTION 1

LESSON 2

Journal entry

How did people respond to the honoring? Again, if you make this a daily pattern, can you see how others will benefit and, ultimately, so will you?

Discussion questions

Discuss the journal topic. Also, discuss how things will begin to change in your life, family, home, job and even community by beginning to put this into practice every day.

_____

_____

_____

_____

_____

_____

_____

_____

Quick thought

If you want further evidence as to whether this idea of honoring others will change your life and the lives around you, think of this: Wouldn't you enjoy having people around you who are more concerned about your needs than they are about their own? Of course you would, and there is your answer.

People are going to want you around as well—simply because your desire is to honor them instead of rip them off. We've all had enough of the rip off.

If you're laboring to help others prosper, of course, they're going to want to see you prosper. Let it become a way of life for you—a daily habit. At first you will have to work at being alert and focusing on honoring others. Eventually, though, it will come from your heart. It will be as natural as breathing. Talk about a bright future—this will do it!

Be POLITE

LESSON 1

LA4 TERM

Similar to honor, politeness is considering the needs of others before our own. It's a way of showing respect toward our fellow human beings—for example, opening the door for others, using good manners (like saying "please" and "thank you" in a respectful tone) and assisting those in need.

And many of you may already practice much of this daily but interestingly enough, the more you think on this the more alert you become to the needs of others. As a result, you'll be even more polite and a stronger person of character.

Quick thought

Everyone wants respect; few, however, want to give it. If you are polite and have good manners, you are showing respect for yourself and others. Ultimately, this is the only way to receive respect from other people. You will begin to shine.

Don't worry about how others treat you. Just treat them the way you like to be treated. Then you have the satisfaction of knowing you're doing your best.

And just like honoring others, ultimately you will receive respect and politeness as well. But only if you are strong enough to stay with it.

© 2000 - 22 TROY... Pure Blue Creative, LLC LA4™

Developing Practical Living Skills - SECTION 1

List some polite habits that you already practice daily

_____
_____
_____
_____
_____
_____
_____
_____
_____

List some areas of politeness in which you need to work on

_____
_____
_____
_____
_____
_____
_____
_____
_____

Life applications

Make an effort to be polite in every way possible both at home and at work.

LA4 – Be Polite

LESSON 2

How did being polite make you feel?

_____
_____
_____
_____
_____
_____
_____

How do you think it made others feel?

_____
_____
_____
_____
_____
_____
_____
_____

Developing Practical Living Skills – SECTION 1

Can you see the benefit of continuing in this behavior at a deeper level? Explain

_____
_____
_____
_____
_____
_____
_____
_____
_____

Discussion questions

Everyone share some interesting experiences that occurred while learning to be more polite. Take note of the interesting experiences of your co-workers.

_____
_____
_____
_____
_____
_____
_____
_____
_____

Journal entry

Why do you suppose so few people practice being polite as a day-to-day habit? How can you make sure you don't fall back into some of those old, lazy ways of being rude and basically inconsiderate?

LA4 – Be Polite

LESSON 3

Quick thought

Like much of what we work on in LA4, it first takes a desire to change and then, of course, the practicing of your new attitudes and ways. And as you continue to practice good habits, slowly but surely they will become part of who you are.

Below, we are going to practice being courteous. So give it all you've got, and it will be that much sooner that you will be a very polite person. Not just a polite person but a successful one. If you use these new skills in your everyday life—whether at home, at work or even out in the community—you will shine!

Activity

[ ] Begin practicing with one another (or with your teacher or within groups) the following:

[ ] Greet with a firm handshake.

[ ] Look the person in the eye while shaking hands.

[ ] Speak clearly; don't mumble while introducing yourself and others.

[ ] Practice introducing others, as well as yourself.

[ ] Practice phrases like "Yes, please," No, thank you" and "Thank you, I would appreciate that very much."

[ ] Help each other by pointing out strengths and weaknesses.

I know this is standard business stuff but it's amazing how sloppy many of us become as the years go by—without even knowing it. Let's dig into the fundamentals and strengthen ourselves a bit. You'll be amazed how your self confidence grows through this. You will begin to notice the difference and so will others.

Journal entry

Can you begin to see how this would impact people and their first impressions of you? Can you also see how you yourself would gain more favor in the business world? In addition, in what situations can you begin to use these stronger skills even more?

SECTION 1

TEAMWORK

LA4 – Teamwork

LESSON 1

TERM — Teamwork is individuals working together for a common good. It's the sharing of talents to accomplish a goal together that could not have been done alone.

Quick thought

This goes along with what we have been talking about quite frequently, and that is: people are great resources. Not only can we benefit others with our talents and abilities, but sometimes it's profitable for us all to come together and share our skills. The best thing that we can do in that situation is honor those other people. And the way we do that is show respect and regard for their abilities, stay out of their way and let them do what they do best.

Another thought is that sometimes on our job, or in the community, we are required to work with someone we don't particularly like or someone whose lifestyle we don't respect. That's OK, we can still honor and appreciate their gifts and work with them for the sake of the job (goal or project) without arguing or lowering our own standards.

Storytime

"I Long to Live in a Neighborhood Again"

Discussion questions

Did you notice that each character in my story is unique? Can you describe some unique people (or friends) from your childhood neighborhood or even present home?

_____
_____
_____
_____
_____
_____
_____

Developing Practical Living Skills – SECTION 1

Did you notice in the story that we all worked together to finish each others' chores? That's teamwork. We worked, and everybody benefitted. As a result, we were able to play our games that much sooner. Have you ever helped a friend or friends in this way where everybody involved benefitted? Describe your role in the project. How did you benefit, and how did everyone else benefit?

_____
_____
_____
_____
_____
_____
_____
_____

A fine example of teamwork is found in the story—the example of me organizing the games, my brother being all-time captain and others having their role as well. For example (not from the story): Kim settled all arguments over the rules because she knew them well. Steve often brought Kool-Aid, and Mikey served others by always chasing the balls that rolled across the street or were out of bounds. Teamwork is using our talents and resources (game balls and Kool-Aid) to benefit everyone involved. What is the skill or talent you have that would or does make a difference in your school, home or work?

_____
_____
_____
_____
_____
_____
_____
_____

LA4 – Teamwork

Are you using it to help others? If yes, how? If no, what can you start doing?

_____
_____
_____
_____
_____
_____

Life applications

Begin to be more alert to others' talents and abilities. Look for ways to honor their giftings and look for opportunities to join your talents with others to accomplish a specific goal—a goal that may benefit them, you or all involved.

> As we grow older, we have a way of letting our differences separate us. It seems we've forgotten that everyone has a part to play. Let's try to remember and work together.

I Long to Live in a Neighborhood Again

Jefferson Place was my neighborhood as a child. What a wonderful world it was, with woods nearby and a creek running through it. But best of all were my neighborhood friends.

Although the homes looked much the same—small ranch houses with evenly cut lawns—its occupants were very different. Across the street lived my best friend and constant companion, Mikey. He was shorter than most third-graders, but he was tougher too. And boy, did he have a passion for baseball. He played shortstop, and he would leap and dive and throw himself at any ball that dared to invade his territory. I also pitied anyone who might get in his way when he was running the bases.

Mikey wasn't perfect, but he wasn't mean either. Just like a lot of boys full of life, he was a bit misunderstood. I remember that Mikey disliked a boy named Ira almost as much as he loved baseball. He never explained why, and I guess I never really asked. Ira was a boy who lived on the corner lot by the creek. One day when he got off the bus, Mikey got off with him—and jumped on him. It took me and the bus driver to pull Mikey off Ira. The bus driver called Mikey's mother that night, and that was the end of the feud—forever.

Steve was another good friend who lived just a few doors down. His dad was Mexican and his mom Amish, or at least she used to be. Steve's dad was cool; he had the admiration of us all when he would cruise his Harley Davidson chopper through the neighborhood. Steve's father also would let us watch him fly his remote-controlled airplane.

Steve's mother wasn't quite as helpful in the "cool" department. One day Steve was forced to get on the school bus with "Dippity-do" on his hair. This would have spelled social ruin for most fourth-grade boys. And sure, we called him "Dippity-do head" for a couple of weeks, but Steve shrugged it off with grace. He was an endearing fellow who told the biggest lies ever heard and then would bet us $5 million that they were the truth. In fact, he still owes me a couple hundred million.

As unique as Steve may sound, Jay had everyone beat. He was as thin as a rail, which was partly due, we were told, to the fact that he was born with an upside-down heart with a hole in it and wasn't expected to live through his teens. But he seemed indifferent to his condition, and we seldom mentioned it.

LA4 - Teamwork

Jay reminded me of a younger, naughtier Abe Lincoln. He stood as tall as any of us, but was only in the second grade. He sported two buck teeth with a tremendous gap between the two. Jay held the neighborhood record for distance spitting, a title he carried with pride. He habitually used foul language, uttering phrases I'd never heard. And if you couldn't find Jay, he was probably down by the creek fishing, an ol' stogie hanging out of his mouth.

Jay was not at all athletic, but his sister Kim was. She was the first girl to play on our Little League baseball team and was a welcome addition to any team. Not only did she play, she made the all-star team two years running. Kim's athletic skills, like most of us, were not limited to baseball, as my neighborhood friends and I played many sports in a nearby empty lot—affectionately known as "the field."

It was here that my brother Todd, Kim's on-again-off-again boyfriend, was always captain. He picked the teams, and when we played football, he'd get down on one knee and draw plays in the dirt. I don't remember anyone ever complaining about him being captain all the time. Every team needs a captain, and he was ours. We understood that.

As for me, I was the kid who organized the games. It wasn't hard. No holiday was too special or time too sacred to call on my neighborhood pals. If someone had chores to do first, we all pitched in for the good of the team.

Somehow as we grow older, we have a way of letting our differences separate us. We seldom rally for the sake of the team. It seems we've forgotten that everyone has a part to play. Let's try to remember and work together— whether it costs us a few extra hours or a few extra dollars. A home, business and community are worth it! Yes, I long to live in a neighborhood again.

Developing Practical Living Skills – SECTION 1

LESSONS 2&3

Quick thought

The bottom line of teamwork is using our abilities to help others, as we have been talking about, but it is also realizing that others have talents, abilities and resources that can be a benefit to us as well if we honor them. If we work together sometimes, we can accomplish a lot more than by ourselves. It starts by appreciating others' talents and abilities as well as our own.

And just think how good it feels when someone encourages you. Others feel the same way when you notice, compliment and honor their talents, giftings or positive character traits.

Group project

If possible, each person should do a two- to five-minute presentation on a talent or skill that he or she has developed. Please bring in materials or props to help people understand. It should be a talent or skill that is unique or at least somewhat unusual.

Journal entry

Discuss some options for your project. Also describe some other talents and skills that you have. Even if they may not be "unique," they are still good and can be a benefit to others.

Follow-up questions to presentations

What can you do to improve the talent or skill that you shared with others?

_____
_____
_____
_____
_____

LA4 – Teamwork

What were some presentations that really impressed you?
_____
_____
_____
_____
_____
_____
_____

What can you do to encourage others in their talents and skills?
_____
_____
_____
_____
_____
_____
_____

LA4 – Express Yourself

LESSON 1

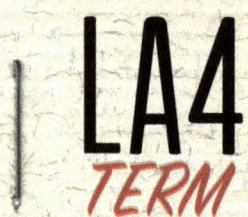

To express is to convey a message that uniquely represents who you are; it can be negative or positive.

Articulation simply means to express your message clearly. You can express in various ways: for example, talking, listening, being thoughtful, writing and even sharing a talent or skill with someone.

Quick thought

Let's be straightforward. Nobody wants to listen to people complain all the time (negative expression). If you have something you need to "get off your chest," try writing in your journal. Go fishing or smack a golf ball around the course. Focus on the positive. That way when you do express yourself, it will be well received.

When you express yourself positively, it will not only benefit others, but you as well. Isn't that what we have been talking about? If we focus on the good of others, it ultimately helps us, too.

Storytime

"Oh, Say Can You See—or at Least Play Guitar"

Discussion questions

Have you had an opportunity to express yourself by sharing a talent or ability? If so, how did it make you feel when you took the risk and did so?

_____
_____
_____
_____

Developing Practical Living Skills – SECTION 1

In my story, I was asked to perform. Have you ever had the opportunity to express through a talent or ability, but you didn't because nobody asked or you didn't volunteer? If yes, please explain.

_____
_____
_____
_____
_____
_____

How could have that situation or performance been even better with your help? (Think this through.) Of course, there are some things and events or even everyday opportunities that would have been better if you had chosen to share talents and positive expression. Just like what my little stint on the guitar did: I improved our class performance. I brought more excitement to my classmates by playing guitar. I benefitted from it as well. I began to feel a pride for the principles that this nation was founded upon—I played with honor. Others may well be missing out by your holding back from expressing yourself positively.

_____
_____
_____
_____
_____

Life applications

Find a safe place to express yourself positively—such as home, club, team or church. Begin to look for opportunities to share your talents or skills with others—both in and out of the workplace.

Expressing yourself positively to benefit others could be seen in many different expressions, not just talents or skills. There are many ways: for instance, laughter (joy), patience or even kindness toward others. These are ways to uplift others while expressing yourself. What's great about these is that you need no special talent. Just choose to do it.

LA4 - Express Yourself

Oh, Say Can You See—or at Least Play Guitar

It was the spring of '76, and I was a sixth-grader at Millersburg Elementary School. Since school wouldn't be in session on July 4, we were having our bicentennial celebration early.

The program was to be a special evening performance in May for parents and community members. One day my role in the program suddenly increased. It was during one of our many practice sessions while singing "America, the Beautiful" that my buddy Greg blurted out, "This is boring . . . every song on piano! We need a rock 'n' roll guitar."

Miss Fields quickly fired back, "And just who, pray tell, will we get? Elvis?"

"No," said Greg calmly. "We'll get Troy."

My mouth dropped open and I looked up at Miss Fields for her usual comeback to Greg's suggestions (which was "say hello to the chalkboard, young man"). But this time, she paused, pondered, then said, "Good idea."

Being a little unsure of myself—having never played in public—my vote was still for Elvis. But after a few moments of "Oh, please" from my classmates and a reassuring grip on the shoulder from my teacher, I was ready to make my debut. After all, I could play every song from my John Denver songbook almost flawlessly.

I brought my guitar (sorry, Greg: acoustic, not electric) to class every day for two weeks. I even practiced at home and was doing all right.

The excitement was mounting as the day approached. In History class, we learned about "Taxation without representation." We also learned about people yearning to live free to worship God as they saw fit—and we learned about courage.

Finally, the night arrived. I put on my red, white and blue bell-bottom pants three hours early, all the while tuning up my six-string. Elvis' loss was my gain, and my gain partially included Becky, who had not paid a whole lot of attention to me until my recent exploits in Music class. When I arrived, she was just as I imagined: red, white and blue bows tied to her pretty pigtails. She walked by me, smiled sweetly and said, "You'll be great!" Normally, this would have been enough to put

Developing Practical Living Skills – SECTION 1

a smile on my face for a week, but this night my mind was filled with something greater, something I couldn't quite put my finger on.

When the lights went down and all of us sixth-graders walked ceremoniously onto the gym floor unfolding a giant banner that read "America's Bicentennial 1776- 1976," my hands began to tremble. It wasn't in fear of the crowd as I had imagined; it was because of pride, a sense of purpose I'd not known before. It isn't easy for a sixth-grader to play guitar accompaniment with dignity, but that night I think I succeeded.

My bell-bottoms have long since worn out, with a solemn promise made that they will never to be worn again, and my John Denver songbook has been left to gather dust in my parents' basement. I hope, though, there's still room in my heart for "America, the Beautiful."

Troy

LA4 – Express Yourself

LESSON 2

Discussion questions

Describe some opportunities that you have coming up that will provide a chance for you to express yourself positively in a way that you have not in the past … keeping in mind that the older we get the more difficult it seems for us to be vulnerable and put ourselves out there—even if it's not playing a rock-n-roll guitar. Just being the only positive person in the room can be tough enough.

_____
_____
_____
_____
_____
_____

How can you prepare for these opportunities?

_____
_____
_____
_____
_____
_____
_____
_____

Developing Practical Living Skills – SECTION 1

How will these special events, performances or everyday life situations be better for others and you if you express yourself positively?

_____
_____
_____
_____
_____
_____
_____

Quick thought

Sometimes the best way to express ourselves and build others up is to do it without worrying or even caring what others' response might be. People can tell when you're "showing off" or when you're just humbly expressing yourself.

I realize that it's hard to just decide, "All right, I don't care what others think;" however, we can practice that attitude simply by taking advantage of every opportunity to express ourselves positively. Just like everything else we have

been talking about, it then becomes a way of life. A much freer life at that.

Life applications

Again, keep looking for that safe place—such as home, club, team or place of worship—to express yourself in a positive way. Look for opportunities to share your talents and skills with others.

And don't forget the best and easiest way—and that is patience, kindness and speaking well of yourself and others. So start expressing. You'll find that others need to experience it as much as you need to share it.

HUMBLE YOURSELF

LESSON 1

Journal entry

Now that we have discussed the topic of self-expression, are you finding ways to express yourself positively? Are you finding some joy and excitement as you share your talents and skills? How will this change your life and the life of others for the better if you continue in the process?

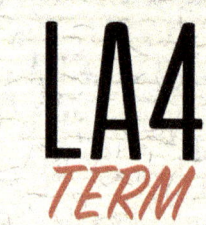

To be humble or walk in humility is a rare quality these days. The best way to understand what humility is may be to first understand what it's not. It isn't pride or arrogance. It is an understanding that we are all just human, no matter how successful or good at something we become or think we've become.

© 2000 - 22 TROY... Pure Blue Creative, LLC LA4™

Developing Practical Living Skills - SECTION 1

To be humble is to treat others with respect. It doesn't worry about protecting some false image. It means being ourselves and not "freaking out" if we are seen in a bad light for a short time.

Quick thought

Humility is freedom. After all, it's a lot of pressure worrying about how you look and how people perceive you. Just think how good it would feel if you let all the junk go—Do your best and try to improve every day. As it relates to business, it won't be long until others, your boss or clients, see the difference.

Storytime

"The Cow Patty Cruiser"

Discussion questions (finish questions during next lesson)

How do you think you would respond if you found yourself with a few cow patties in your face?

_____
_____
_____
_____
_____
_____

Has something this embarrassing every happened to you? If so, what was it?

_____
_____
_____
_____
_____

LA4 - Humble Yourself

How did you respond?
_____
_____
_____
_____
_____

How would you respond differently now?
_____
_____
_____
_____
_____

Do you have a friend like my buddy Roger who would just laugh with you and not at you—then get the hose? Are you a friend like that?
_____
_____
_____
_____
_____
_____
_____

the Cow Patty Cruiser

It was in the fall of my fifth-grade year when I managed to get my dream machine: a minibike. This one came directly from my neighbor, Terry, who had entered junior high school and felt he was now too old for the minibike of his youth.

The homemade machine was a bargain beauty at $40 (money I had saved from mowing a few lawns). It had a mighty 3 1/2-horsepower engine set in a standard bar frame, but that was just about its only traditional feature. Since Terry's mother was a seamstress, she made the seat and it was a masterpiece of construction. A foot thick and softer than any pillow I'd ever sat on, the seat was nearly a yard long and, like my father's LTD Country Squire station wagon, could comfortably seat a family of six. Well, close to it anyway.

The 12 inches of foam had me riding high in the saddle, which may have looked a little odd since I was tall and thin, and it left me reaching down for the throttle. But that didn't bother me. I named her the "Comfort Cruiser," and we went everywhere together.

We rode the trails by the railroad tracks, kicked up dust on the country roads and buzzed around the barn when I was bored. But my favorite place to ride was the Millers' place next door. They had a field behind their shed where their son Roger and I had worn down an oval racetrack.

Roger and I enjoyed a good race. He rode a homemade three-wheeler that his dad had built. I, of course, piloted the "Cruiser."

Despite the challenges of the course, Roger handled his craft with skill. Though a mild-mannered young man, he wasn't afraid to bump up next to me at top speed. Challenges included the three or four cows that grazed within our oval. Besides the obvious obstacles that the cows daily deposited on our track were the cows themselves who, believe it or not, liked

to play "chicken."

As we'd speed down the straight-aways, one or two of the cows would occasionally run down the path directly toward us. And since cows are not known for being quick-footed, we'd often have to veer to our right off the smooth trail and onto the bumpy field. One thing we soon discovered is that the cows always turned to their right as we got closer. As a result, the cows seldom slowed us down. After a while, they would stay in the middle of the oval and stand there with annoyed looks on their faces. (I guess cows always have annoyed looks on their faces.)

LA4 – Humble Yourself

I remember one autumn afternoon in particular when Roger and I were racing. The cows started out with their game of cow-chicken, but we ignored them, going on with our competition. As usual, the cows tired of the sport and opted for the middle of the oval. But as we started our last lap, the cows would have the last laugh.

I was right on Roger's tail as we entered the last curve. He was going so fast that his right-rear wheel came off the ground, spinning frantically. When the wheel came down, it landed on a fresh cow patty, shooting it directly back onto me . . . SPLAT! SPLAT! SPLAT!

With Roger going on to victory, I skidded to a disoriented halt. My bare chest was covered and a few fragments had caught my neck and cheek as well.

A few minutes later, in Roger's backyard, we laughed uncontrollably while he hosed me and my minibike down, now dubbed the "Cow Patty Cruiser."

As I look back and smile, I hope that if something out of the ordinary, something humbling, happens to me or you (whether at school, work or play), in the spirit of two young boys we can roll on the ground in laughter while a friend gets the hose.

Troy

Developing Practical Living Skills – SECTION 1

LESSON 2

Discussion questions

If needed, take some time now to finish questions from Lesson 1.

_____
_____
_____
_____

Quick thought

Humbling yourself, like everything else we're talking about, is a choice. Interestingly enough, few make that choice. Often the reason is wanting to "be somebody." So many people strut around wanting others to notice them, but seldom does anybody notice because they're too busy doing the same thing themselves.

Is that silly or what? It's true, isn't it? If you truly humble yourself—you can't fake it—you'll shine like the noonday sun. It's such a refreshing change these days. Can you see the freedom of being yourself and letting others do the same?

If others want to play the game, let ém. But for those who want more, put a smile on your face, let the cow patties fall where they may, and get out there and enjoy. Life is good.

Journal entry

Can you truly say that you humble yourself? Your family, your boss and even those who work under your authority could most likely tell you. What would they say?

Just because someone says, "Oh, I'm no good at anything," it doesn't mean that they're humble. It means they are a "pouty pants." We have heard enough of that kind of whining and done enough of it ourselves—move on! Ironically, it sometimes takes just as much humility to say "that's not too high for me" as it does to say, "that's not too low."

So as you write in your journal, devise a plan. Humility is a daily choice. But first we have to be willing to admit that we are doing something wrong and change it. That, my friend, is humility.

Let's GET ORGANIZED

LESSON 1

LA4 TERM — Organize simply means to put in order. If you have a collection of books, you would put them in the same place every time after use. This is organization. It saves time and effort. You can organize your time, your office or even your garage. The list goes on and on.

Quick thought

Think of how many times you couldn't find something—something that you use frequently. Or, ever tell a friend that you would meet him or her somewhere only to forget later? The problem: you are unorganized. It takes only a few moments of planning to save hours and hours (not to mention embarrassment). Believe it or not, most people (adults) and many businesses are very much unorganized.

© 2000 - 22 TROY... Pure Blue Creative, LLC LA4™

Like the many other concepts that LA4 teaches, if you can grab hold of this concept, you will certainly have an advantage that most folks don't have. The best way to begin is by organizing one of your most precious resources—time.

Daily planner tips

A planner is a good way to get organized—digital or good, ole' fashioned paper. Purchasing one now will help you with this curriculum. With your daily planner you can begin organizing immediately. Some tips include:

- Always have your planner with you or nearby. This is important so that you can write down appointments or meetings right away so that you don't forget them.

- Begin your day just 10 minutes earlier by looking over your list for the day, making notes and even looking a few days ahead to get a feel for where you're going. This 10 minutes will ultimately save you hours and hours of trouble, not to mention the stress and pressure you'll be free of by starting the day organized.

- Set goals and deadlines. If you don't complete a project, then make sure you write it down on the next day's schedule. This will keep you from putting things off. Eventually, you'll get tired of writing that undone item every day, and you'll just get it done.

- It's also a good idea to take a few moments during the day (if possible the same time each day) and look over your schedule again. Check off the activities you have completed and make plans to complete the others. If something needs to be altered, this is an excellent time to make adjustments.

You'll be amazed at how much time most of us waste during the day. If you are faithful, your income as well as free time will increase.

LESSON 2

Journal entry

Discuss areas in your life that will be more organized and run more smoothly by using your planner. Also, describe why this daily habit could change your life for the good as you continue to work on it and improve.

Quick thought

When you organize your time as we discussed earlier, not only do you begin to see how much time has been wasted, you have an opportunity to do something about it. This, of course, will give you more time to do other things.

LA4 – Let's Get Organized

Many people buy into the lie that being unorganized or just doing what they want is freedom. That's not freedom—it's chaos. It's only when we are organized and really have an understanding of what is going on do we have the freedom to make good choices. Otherwise, we do very little and go nowhere.

Another example of this would be money. If you develop a simple budget, you will begin to see that much money (like time) is wasted and, with a little organization, you can do so much more. Below are just a few things. Make your own list. It's a documented fact that folks that make more money than the "average" have just as many money "issues" as those who make less.

Funny, years ago, my wife and I used envelopes each titled like the areas in the chart below. We would cash our paychecks, put some money in the bank and then distribute the cash to the appropriate envelope. For example, if the entertainment envelope was empty five days prior to our next paycheck then too bad. It was not fun at times but it taught us discipline and paid off big time—within a short amount of time, we were able to purchase our first home.

Budget development

Average Income Per Week

- Your Income _____
- Spouse Income _____
- Other _____
  - total Income _____

Average Expenses Per Week

- Housing _____
- Car(s) _____
- Childcare _____
- Groceries _____
- Entertainment _____
- Utilities/Bills _____
- Donations _____
- All Other _____
  - total Expenses _____

Income vs. Expenses (income minus expenses)

- total income _____
- total expenses − _____
- Net Excess (Loss) _____

© 2000 - 22 TROY... Pure Blue Creative, LLC LA4™

Developing Practical Living Skills – SECTION 1

The chart on the preceding page is just an outline. Now, make a chart that fits your situation.

Average Income Per Week

_____ $ _____
_____ $ _____
_____ $ _____
_____ $ _____
_____ $ _____
_____ $ _____

total income _____

Average Expenses Per Week

_____ $ _____
_____ $ _____
_____ $ _____
_____ $ _____
_____ $ _____
_____ $ _____
_____ $ _____
_____ $ _____
_____ $ _____

total expenses _____

total income $ _____ minus total expnses $ _____

Net Excess or (Loss) $ _____

Discussion questions

What are your two most expensive items? Is there any way to cut the cost or frequent use?

_____
_____
_____
_____
_____
_____
_____

LA4 – Let's Get Organized

What are some things that you would like to save money for but up to this point you have not been able?

_____
_____
_____
_____
_____
_____
_____

Look at your chart and begin to devise a plan to save money and make more money if needed.

_____
_____
_____
_____
_____
_____
_____
_____
_____
_____

SECTION 1

Commit to EXCELLENCE

LESSON 1

Journal entry

Discuss the principle of managing your time and money. Focus on the fact that the more you organize your time and money the more you are able to take advantage of the extra money and extra time.

LA4 TERM — Excellence is a condition of superiority. It's tops. Nothing better. It's not always perfect; therefore, it is an obtainable goal.

LA4 – Commit to Excellence

Quick thought

Excellence is something that we often hear of but seldom see. You can be a person of excellence simply by working hard and doing your very best.

Don't get excellence confused with perfectionism. Perfectionism (thinking that you have to do everything perfectly) is a lie. You are going to make mistakes, and that's OK; mistakes can be useful. They show us what works and what doesn't. Excellence is a commitment to doing your personal best. Not just "good enough" or "acceptable" but best.

Excellence is understanding the difference between the act of failing and being a failure. Problems will always exist, but instead of being angry and frustrated, a person of excellence sees problems as an opportunity for a solution.

There is no shame in making mistakes. It's only when we don't learn from those mistakes that there's a problem.

An attitude of a failure is being afraid to make mistakes or admit that a mistake was made. So do your best. Work hard, and if you make a few mistakes or even a lot of them, SO WHAT! At least you're doing something.

Own up to your mistakes (that's humility, and it will bring respect and favor). Learn from your mistakes—move on—and you will succeed.

Discussion questions

What are some mistakes that you've made more than once? How would you handle those situations differently now?

_____
_____
_____
_____
_____
_____
_____
_____

Developing Practical Living Skills – SECTION 1

What are some mistakes that you have made but learned from?

_____
_____
_____
_____
_____
_____
_____
_____

Are you doing your best at work, home, everywhere? How can you do better to be a person of excellence? What specific changes need to be made?

_____
_____
_____
_____
_____
_____
_____
_____
_____
_____

Section 1: Summary

LESSON 1

Quick thought

The bottom line to this first section, and really LA4 as a whole, is honoring those in authority. And it's treating everyone as you yourself would like to be treated. It sounds simple, and it is. But as we found out in this section, there is a lot to it, and it will take a great deal of effort on your part to continue to improve.

But you can do it, and the rewards are great. But this program is not for the wimps or whiners. It is for the courageous and the strong. People like some of you who are willing to look at your faults, face them and change.

If you're with me so far, and you're beginning to practice things like honoring others, being polite, expressing yourself in a positive manner, humbling yourself, being organized and committing yourself to excellence, you're well on your way to an even more successful and enjoyable life. And these next sections will really send you sailing

SUMMARY OF SECTION

For the following practical living skills that we developed in this section, define the term and explain some ways in which you are now using these skills to a greater level and how they are changing your day-to-day life.

Honoring others

_____
_____
_____
_____
_____

© 2000 - 22 TROY... Pure Blue Creative, LLC LA4™

Developing Practical Living Skills – SECTION 1

Being polite

Expressing yourself in a positive manner

Humbling yourself

LA4 - Summary

Being organized

_____
_____
_____
_____

Committing yourself to excellence

_____
_____
_____
_____

How I made up my mind to change, and how I will work at it

_____
_____
_____
_____

© 2000 - 22 TROY... Pure Blue Creative, LLC LA4™

Developing Practical Living Skills – SECTION 1

LESSON 2

Review of section

Finish review questions from previous lesson

Discussion questions

Share some of your answers from the section review with others. Listen to theirs.

Journal entry

Of all that was studied in this section, what part of LA4 has made the biggest difference in your life and why? Please explain.

LIFE APPLICATION 2

Building Strength of CHARACTER

LESSON 1

> **1 LA4 TERM** — Character is doing the right thing at the right time regardless of what others may do or say.

To be strong in character you must first understand what's right or true. Truth is that which conforms to reality. In other words, it's those things that are undeniable or do not change. We witness many truths every day. For example, gravity—when is the last time you dropped a water glass or a bowling ball and it didn't go straight to the floor?

Well, of course it did. It's gravity, and no matter how many times you drop that bowling ball, you'd better watch your toes.

That's what is so great about truth. You can count on it just like you can count on the sun coming up every morning. But truth goes well beyond just nature and facts. There are truths, and there are lies. We have all told lies and have been lied to. Why do people lie? To cover or hide the truth … to avoid an uncomfortable reality.

If you argue that the sun does not come up every morning, you may get a few people to believe you; however, will this change the truth? Of course not. Will they eventually discover that you lied? More than likely.

© 2000 - 22 TROY… Pure Blue Creative, LLC LA4™

Building Strength of Character – SECTION 2

Quick thought

As we begin to accept truth and live by it the best we can, we develop strong character because we don't have to worry about someone finding out the truth.

Lazy people lie. Those with strength and a future love the truth. Liars never prosper for long. Those who love truth prosper and become the strength of communities. They are the type of people whom others look to in times of trouble—the type of people whom others go to for answers they can trust.

Another thing you may notice about someone who is strong in character is that he does what he says or tells others to do. In other words, people of character "practice what they preach."

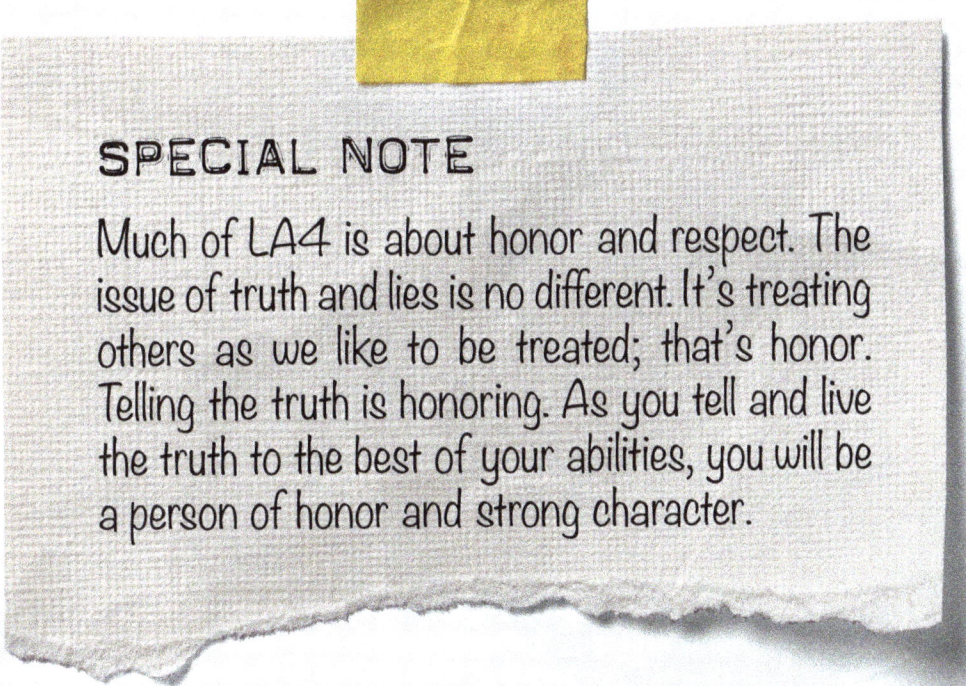

SPECIAL NOTE

Much of LA4 is about honor and respect. The issue of truth and lies is no different. It's treating others as we like to be treated; that's honor. Telling the truth is honoring. As you tell and live the truth to the best of your abilities, you will be a person of honor and strong character.

Journal entry

Discuss a time or two that you lied to hide the truth. Also, discuss the times that others have lied to you. How much better would things have been if everyone just told the truth in those situations?

Journal entry 2

Can you see how living and loving truth make you strong? Explain. In addition, describe how lying can make you weak and untrustworthy.

LETTER OF THE LAW

LESSON 1

LA4 TERM

Law brings order. It is the foundation. Law enforces truth. It is the structure—like railroad tracks. To some, the tracks may seem limiting, but without them the train is useless. Without law there is chaos. There must be rules, and those rules must be followed.

As soon as you come to terms with that, there is freedom within those laws. Everything else is left to us. The train, for example, is free to do what it was made to do. It can speed up. It can slow down. It can pull a few cars or many—just as you will be free to be creative and express yourself in many positive ways, provided you stay within the boundaries of the law. You'll be amazed how much room there is to move and grow within the letter of the law. And you will have the security of knowing that what you are doing is right.

If you are constantly trying to push or step over the line of the law, that is not freedom, only fear: fear of getting caught and fear of punishment. Not to mention the unsettled feeling you get because you know you're doing something wrong. There is no joy or peace in that: you must accept basic law.

Another simple example of the purpose and necessity for law would be sports and other games. Without rules, we would have no games. Think of basketball. Without rules, would anybody dribble? Wouldn't you knock someone over every time he tried to shoot the ball? But with the rules, we can enjoy dunks and three-pointers, spin moves and behind-the-back dribbles. Are you beginning to see the importance of law (rules)? And also freedom?

© 2000 - 22 TROY... Pure Blue Creative, LLC LA4™

Building Strength of Character – SECTION 2

Quick thought

You might wonder why our second lesson in the Strength of Character section is on law. Well, in order to walk with character and integrity we first must develop an understanding and an appreciation for law. There has to be a line drawn that we will not cross. That will be our railroad tracks. Without them, we have nothing to guide us.

Let's start with a look at some rules (or laws) that we had as kids. Rules that maybe we didn't understand but later discovered, the hard way, that were there for our own good. You see, laws are neither for us nor against us. They are there to bring order. Those who learn to follow them prosper, those who don't follow them won't prosper at all—or at least not for very long.

Storytime

Sweet Potato Pants

It was August of 1970, and I was to be a first-grader in elementary school. Ah, first grade, school all day . . . lunch on a tray. I couldn't wait!

At first, lunch was all I'd dreamed it would be—food, friends and laughter. How I loved the lunch tray built with little sections for each food group. Because at six years of age, one thing you know is that food should never mingle with other food.

My favorite entree was the green Jell-O. It was fun, full of flavor, and it could fly . . . well, at least with the help of a hard puff through a straw. There was something wonderful about the way Jell-O wobbles in mid-air, almost as if in slow motion, and then—splat!—as it strikes its target with full force. This went on for a short time before I misfired at Jason Bobie and landed one just short of Miss Buller's foot. She handled it well, just before she "handled" the scruff of my neck into the kitchen where my sentence was quick and just—one week of cafeteria clean-up during recess.

Sure, I missed a whole week of dodge ball and kick ball, but I was guilty, and the punishment fit the crime. Soon, with lesson learned, lunchtime was fun again . . . until that day of the dreaded orange dish—sweet potatoes.

I knew that anything that color should never meet my lips. That's one of the great things about being a kid: You need only to see the food article to judge its taste. Two lumps surrounded by a moat. Oozy and orange.

LA4 – Letter of the Law

As I carried my tray back to the clean-up line, blood rushed to my face, and I began to sweat, remembering the rule: "You must try everything on your plate." Quickly, I stirred up my cold, lumpy sweet potatoes in hopes of fooling Miss Buller, but she was a cafeteria veteran and that old trick wasn't going to work. "Take a bite of that sweet potato," she said calmly. Her stern persistence got the bite to my mouth, but no sooner had it entered than it shot back, unceremoniously, to the tray.

From that day on, the fear of this food ruined lunchtime for me. I had to find a way to hide those potatoes. At first, I would heave a helping under the table, which worked until I hit Joey Wattenberger on the leg— then it was back to KP duty. One day I stumbled upon the solution: the milk carton. It was perfect. I always scrunched my carton down anyway, so why not shovel a few spoonfuls of sweet potato into the carton first?

This carried me through winter and most of spring, until I got a little careless one day and left a dab on top of the carton. Miss Buller had me open the carton and there it was: lumpy and, by now, mixed with milk. Proud of her discovery, she happily handed me a spoon and said, "I want to see a big bite now."

What happened next is still a blur, but I knew I was in trouble. With just a few weeks of school remaining, I had exhausted all my options, my sane ones anyway.

The fateful day came the last week of school. I sat there silently as time ticked away. With all hope lost, I took a heaping spoonful, opened my front-left pocket, and shoved it in. Math class was miserable as I felt the warmth of the sweet potato against my leg. Even as the gloppy mess cooled, my stomach was every bit as queasy as if I'd eaten it.

Looking back, I know Miss Buller was trying to help me build strong bones and character, but I guess all of us, one way or another, must learn from our Sweet Potato Pants.

Building Strength of Character – SECTION 2

Discussion questions

Sure, blowing Jell-O through a straw was fun for a while; however, if everybody would have been allowed to do that, lunch would have been chaos, and only a few would have been able to enjoy their lunchtime. Can you think of a rule that you broke as a child but now realize why the rule was in place? Please describe.

_____

_____

_____

_____

_____

_____

_____

If I hadn't been punished for blowing and throwing food, would I have ever stopped? Probably not. They could have talked to me every day, but until I got KP duty, I was going to keep doing it. Please describe a time when you broke a rule and were punished and, as a result, you never broke that rule again.

_____

_____

_____

_____

_____

_____

_____

_____

LA4 – Letter of the Law

LESSON 2

Discussion questions

Can you see the importance of punishing a lawbreaking act? Please explain your answer.

_____
_____
_____
_____
_____
_____

Just as I went through much trauma and grief by trying to avoid just one or two bites of those potatoes, can you think of a time when you tried to sneak past the rules, like I did, and ended up miserable? Only to find out later that it would have been much easier to just follow the rules or instructions. Please describe.

_____
_____
_____
_____
_____

Miss Buller was just doing her job. Do you think she enjoyed hearing kids complain? The easiest thing for her to do would have been to let the kids go and not really check their lunch trays. She checked because she was doing the job for which she was paid and because she saw the big picture; she wanted kids to quit "wimping out" and be brave enough to try something new.

_____
_____
_____
_____

Building Strength of Character – SECTION 2

Journal entry

Discuss some situations where others don't follow the rules and why it makes you mad. Also, be honest with yourself and discuss at least one situation where you break the rules, and it makes others mad and causes some chaos.

Life applications

Begin to be more alert to areas where people cross the line of the law and how it makes you feel. At the same time, be honest with yourself and examine the areas of the law that you've crossed. You may have felt that it was OK because it was you and not someone else. Begin to look for opportunities to change those old patterns.

If you need motivation, just think how upset you get at others when they break the rules; however, others have good reason to be annoyed with you, too. And remember as a person of strong character, you don't point out the fault of someone else unless you yourself have already taken care of that same issue.

Even if you have overcome a specific issue, it's generally wise to keep quiet and save your advice for those who ask for it. When you're quick to improve your own problems and slow to point out everybody else's, you'll be amazed at how people will start asking you for advice.

> Constantly trying to step over the line of the law is not freedom, only fear; fear of getting caught and fear of punishment.

Be a LEADER

LESSON 1

> **LA4 TERM**
> To be a leader one first must learn to follow—you follow by (and here it is again) first honoring those in authority.

Honor is the key to almost all that we discuss in LA4—leadership is no exception. In fact, without honor and respect, there is no possible way to be a good leader or a follower.

First, as a follower, we must honor those in authority by doing what we are told without argument or complaint. Our efforts should be focused on seeing those in leadership prosper.

Interestingly enough, to be a leader is not much different—only you have more responsibility. A good leader honors those who work under him or her by laboring to see them improve and prosper: an encouraging word at just the right time, a rebuke when needed to keep them on the right track and, most of all, a live example of excellence.

A leader also sets goals for the "team" and individuals and labors with all to help them get there. Strong leaders don't lord over, they build up.

© 2000 - 22 TROY... Pure Blue Creative, LLC LA4™

Building Strength of Character – SECTION 2

Quick thought

Without a healthy respect for truth, law and order (as mentioned in the previous lessons), there is no way anyone can be an effective leader. This is true across the board from Boy Scout/Girl Scout leader to factory manager to president of the United States. Without this strength of character, the person in leadership is too prone to weakness and mistakes.

As for good leaders, there are very few. But know this: You can be a good leader, and you can start working on these skills immediately. First, as already mentioned, work on honoring and respecting those who have a great deal of responsibility. Nothing could ever prepare you better for being a leader than working on these traits.

And second, be alert to those in authority over you now. Even if they aren't great leaders, they still may have some skills you can learn from. So be alert and notice those qualities.

You can be a great leader someday soon—if you're not already that is, and maybe it will be as a leader in business, government or your community. You don't have to be in a "big" position to be a successful leader, just a good example who points others in the right direction. But one thing is sure: If you can learn this and live it, the world needs you desperately. There are too few people who understand honor and true leadership.

Discussion questions

Discuss someone you know whom you consider a solid leader. Discuss some qualities that this person has that you appreciate and why.

_____

_____

_____

Think of a teacher, coach, boss or parent whom you admire. What did they say and do that clearly demonstrates that they care or cared about your future and your success?

_____

_____

_____

_____

Journal entry

What qualities do you now have that will make you a good leader? What can you do to improve areas that would weaken you as a leader?

Think UNIQUE

LESSON 1

> **LA4 TERM** — We are all made a little different from each other. It's when we are not strong in character that we work hard at hiding our unique qualities.

People who aren't strong in character also criticize those who are unique. It seems that uniqueness makes others feel uncomfortable. It scares them.

I have funny-looking ears. They look like little dishes or cups. I got teased a lot when I was a kid. But I wouldn't trade them for anything now. Why? Well, I don't know anyone else who has ears like mine. People remember me after they meet me. If not for any other reason, they remember my ears. That's fine with me. (Besides, my wife says they are more lovable—I believe her!)

When we are strong in character, we can appreciate those little differences—in others and in ourselves. How boring would it be if we all drove red mini vans? Then why in the world do we expect others to look like us and think like us? And do the same boring things?

© 2000 - 22 TROY... Pure Blue Creative, LLC LA4™

Building Strength of Character – SECTION 2

The only way I can truly be free to be uniquely me is to have the strength of character to let others be unique without criticizing them for it.

Quick thought

Strength of character is very helpful when it comes to being unique. We can freely be ourselves without fear and without feeling pressure from others. (Remember our expression section?) This strength will enable you to enjoy life much more—appreciate others' differences in tastes and ideas while having the freedom to enjoy your

Be free to enjoy uniqueness, both in yourself and in other people. Let that creativity shine—no more being pushed where you really don't want to go just to fit in with the crowd.

Storytime

"First Day of School and a Furry Bathroom Rug"

Discussion questions

Sometimes, as with the case with my furry rug, we have something or must do something that others think is a little different, and they choose to make fun of it. Has this happened to you? If so, please describe.

_____
_____
_____
_____
_____

Have you made fun of others for being different or unique? If so, what was the situation? How would you handle it differently now?

_____
_____
_____
_____
_____

LA4 - Think Unique

Did having the unique nap mat (furry rug) hurt my relationship with other kids? Why or why not?

_____

_____

_____

_____

First Day of School and a Furry Bathroom Rug

As school reopens each year, I think of the excitement of students entering a new grade and the anticipation of those starting school for the first time.

I remember my first day of school in '69. Because my mother was a teacher and was busy preparing for school herself, we didn't get all my supplies together until that very morning.

While we were racing around the house, we found the paste, scissors and some broken crayons. The crayons had rubbed together so often it was hard to tell the original colors. Finally, we came to the last item on the list—the nap mat.

This seemed to puzzle my mother. For a moment she pondered, then dashed into the bathroom and picked up the lime-colored, furry rug that almost every American has lying on the floor next to the bathtub. With the sack of supplies in my hand, she draped the furry rug over my shoulder and hustled me out the door, where I took that fateful leap onto the big Blue Bird bus.

When I arrived safely at school, I expected to see my fellow classmates with big furry rugs hoisted over their shoulders . . . maybe one would have white, another blue or maybe red. Shoot! Not a furry rug in sight.

While kids stared at me, I realized what was "kindergarten hip" and what wasn't. A little boy named Artie was strutting around with what appeared to be a briefcase, but with a flip of the wrist, it sprung into a beautiful multi-colored nap mat. Boy, was I jealous! Another child had a pack of crayons with 487 colors and an electric sharpener that was so large she had to pull it on wheels and carry an extension cord around to use it.

The day, however, improved. The teacher was nice and we colored. But during the introduction to show-and- tell, we were on our nap mats (my furry rug) when little Jimmy chirped, "Maybe next show-and-tell Troy could bring his matching toilet seat cover."

Hey, that's okay! A few weeks later, when milk and cookies didn't agree with me, I threw up all over little Jimmy's lap. Oh, and that furry rug. Well, as our nap pattern developed, it was "lights out" right after recess. Funny thing about those multi-colored nap mats that come in a briefcase—they're made of hard plastic. Combine that surface with sweaty skin and it's not a pleasant sensation. Soon they were calling out to me, "Hey, you wanna swap?"

Like an actor in a commercial, I propped my hands behind my head and said, "No thanks, guys. I feel good!"

I knew it was gonna be a great year.

LA4 – Think Unique

LESSON 2

Activity

Take a few moments and write down something unique that you appreciate about a few people with whom you work daily. Write each comment on a separate piece of paper and sign it.

Discussion questions

If you're doing this as a group, after everyone has had a few moments to silently read the comments from others, discuss some things that surprised you. Maybe even share one of your own "furry rug" stories.

_____
_____
_____
_____
_____
_____
_____
_____
_____
_____

Life applications

Begin to enjoy the uniqueness of the way you think or look or do certain things. Also, be strong enough in character not to be threatened by other people's differences.

Section 2: Summary

LESSONS 1&2

Quick thought

Character is doing the right thing at the right time. It's "practicing what you preach." All this ties into two other LA4 topics: truth and law and order. Some people like to sit around stroking their chin, acting like they're being profound by saying, "Oh, what is truth?" They don't really care. If they did, they would be pursuing truth, living and loving truth instead of sitting around talking about it.

You have that opportunity now to begin living and loving truth at a much deeper level every day. You can speak truth to the best of your understanding and begin to look for what's right, and you'll find it. If you do that, you are already becoming a person of strong character.

Your journey to truth will take strength as well, simply because when you're doing your best to live and speak truth, sometimes things get a little messy. That's OK. However, there will be plenty of people happy to criticize you for your efforts. That only confirms that you're on the right track. They want to see you fail because they don't have what it takes to pursue truth. Keep pushin'. Remember: It's the lazy who lie—and it's easy to be a critic.

In addition, don't forget the "railroad tracks" of the law. They bring order and freedom and even more strength of character. Enjoy their structure and begin to function within those rules (or laws).

Finally, mix all that with the No. 1 quality—honor—and you're on your way to walking in strength of character … at a level few ever obtain—a person others can count on in tough times. There are just not that many people out there like that. Rise up and be one—you're desperately needed.

Lesson from the barnyard

Turkeys sit and gobble, chickens pick and peck, but eagles soar. It's time for you to fly.

LA4 - Summary

Discussion questions

What are some areas where you are strong in truth?

_____
_____
_____
_____
_____
_____

What are some areas in which you still lie to get your way or avoid dealing with reality?

_____
_____
_____
_____
_____

Are you willing to give up these lies? If so, how are you going to change? Plan a course of action.

_____
_____
_____
_____
_____
_____

Building Strength of Character – SECTION 2

Can you see how walking in truth with a healthy respect for law and order will help you become a person whom others will want to be around and trust even more?

_____
_____
_____
_____
_____

Are you strong enough in character to even give up a few friends who refuse to respect your desire to speak truth and honor law and order? If so, you are well on your way to being considered a man or woman who is strong in character.

_____
_____
_____
_____
_____
_____

Journal entry

Discuss how your life and friends will change as you begin to live truth and love law and order. (And as for those friends you may lose, don't worry, even more friends, friends of honor, are around the corner for people like you who are developing strength of character.)

Journal entry 2

How much better do you feel about yourself as you begin to work harder at speaking truth and honoring law and order?

LIFE APPLICATION 3

LESSON 1

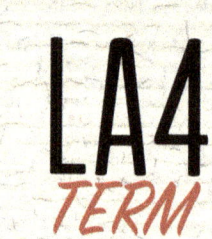

Like everything else we have been talking about, life is a series of choices, and what you put in your mind is a choice as well. What we think about all day long can be changed if we choose.

In this section and in this very lesson, I will offer several suggestions and reasons for changing your thought patterns.

The purpose is not to tell you what to think or how to think but just bring to your attention things that you are doing (thinking) that are lies, junk or just plain a waste of time—thoughts that hinder you from success.

You've heard it said that you are what you eat. In essence, that is true. If someone were to literally eat garbage, it wouldn't be long before it would be evident in many ways, the first being the mouth. He or she would open up to speak, and the stink would roll out and knock you over. The same is true with what you think.

Eventually, what you think will show up in your words—then your emotions and actions as well.

Many believe that one's thoughts are private and hidden, but it won't be long before all of them are clear for all to see; most already are. The good part of that is if you are thinking positive things about yourself and others, about situations and even creative ideas that help others, then that also will be evident.

As you think positively and do positive things, you will certainly become a positive person as well, and there just are not many people like that out there. But you can be one of them simply by being careful and alert to what your mind feeds on.

Quick thought

So obviously, the best way to change what you say, feel and do would be to start changing what you think. You see, right now there are many negative things that you focus on in your mind every day that are hindering you from success. You can change that now!

In the first two sections we were thinking about and focusing on the positive, and that's excellent. The bottom line is you were and are changing patterns in your life that were destructive to patterns of success. If we are going to go a little farther down the road of success, there are other negative patterns that need to be broken. Almost all of these negative patterns start right there in your head.

Life applications

As strange as it may sound, start listening or paying attention to what your mind is telling you. If it is a lie, something negative or just nonsense, then kick it out and focus on something good, hopeful and positive about others, yourself or various situations.

Start listening to your thoughts (in other words, be alert!) while with your friends, when you're mind is wondering during a boring meeting, at home during supper or even as you lie in bed at night—pay attention to those thoughts. You will be amazed at what you find in your own head.

The first step in changing any bad pattern is recognizing it. Then comes the big question: Do you want it changed badly enough to do something about? If the answer is "Yes," then be strong and start kicking out those bad thoughts.

In fact, if you are focusing your thoughts on one or two specific things most of the time, chances are it's something harmful that either needs to be cut way back, or it's something that needs to be kicked out altogether. This will then free up that much more time to focus on positive things—things of life and success.

In keeping with one of the main themes of LA4, it takes effort and alertness to change, but if you are willing to do this, and let it become a habit, you are guaranteeing yourself success. You will become a positive person, and you are much needed. So, out with the bad and in with the good. Let's go!

FEAR IS FAILURE

LESSON 1

Journal entry

Pinpoint some negative thoughts that you realized you were focusing on in your head. Write some alternatives to those thoughts. Give examples of positive things, good things that you can think about instead. And remember that "positive" is anything that works for the good of others, as well as yourself.

For example, think about opportunities to be helpful, to encourage and to find the good in situations that others only complain about. Isn't there enough complaining around? Let's think on the good things and then speak about them. As you learn to do this, your presence becomes priceless.

LA4 TERM

Fear is an expectation of the worst situation; it's often nonsense! It, too, is an issue of what you choose to think about. The problem with fear, like many other thoughts that people choose, is that it eventually shows up in words, emotions and actions. Many studies suggest that at least 80 percent of what most people think about is negative and/or fear based.

Clearing the Clutter – SECTION 3

As mentioned in our previous section, one way to avoid most fear is to do what's right; not cheating, lying or loafing on the job. That alone will save you all kinds of torment from fear. There is very little rest, peace or enjoyment when fear is dominating your thoughts. It's true!

However, there are other types of fear that people choose every day. As a result, they end up reacting, saying and doing things that lead to failure. A good example is control. When people fear, they control in any way possible. They try to control situations and other people as well.

And what are they really afraid of? They're afraid things are not going to come out their way. In other words, it's their selfish desires that lead to this type of fear and control. They want what they want, and they will get it any way they can. They're never satisfied. People who get away with controlling others only want to control to an even greater degree next time. If that's you, it's time to change.

We can't stop others from fearing and trying to control us. However, we can stop acting that way ourselves and more quickly recognize when people try to do that to us. True friends do not control one another, they honor. Control is dishonor, and if a "friend" is doing that to you, simply walk away. If this person continues in that, he is not really a friend.

Discussion questions

Discuss some of the many things that people do out of fear.

_____
_____
_____
_____
_____
_____

Be brave and bold and admit a time or two that you have tried to control others out of fear.

_____
_____
_____
_____
_____
_____
_____

LA4 - Fear is Failure

Are there any situations where you can acknowledge that you constantly try to control? Are you willing to give up this behavior for the sake of success? If so, what will you do differently in that situation?

___

Discuss how good it would feel if we just let all that ride and work hard and trust. Freedom comes when we don't lie or cheat or become lazy; freedom also comes when we work hard do our best and don't worry about getting our way. Trust that good things will happen even though it might take some time to see good results.

SECTION 3

Prejudice is to PREJUDGE

LESSON 1

Journal entry

Now that you have a better idea of what fear does to lead you to failure, discuss some of your old fear patterns and begin to devise a plan to get rid of that fear. Also, please mention the freedom and success you are beginning to see as a result of getting rid of those fears.

LA4 TERM

As we were just discussing, fear is often nonsense, and fear often promotes prejudice. We as human beings frequently fear things we don't understand or that are different from our day-to-day experiences.

Sometimes the result of seeing things in this light is prejudice. Prejudice means to prejudge. In other words, it means to make up your mind about a person, group of people or situation without all the facts.

LA4 – Prejudice is to Prejudge

Quick thought

Why is there so much prejudice? It's easy to do. It's easy to think the worst about most people. It's easy to be angry. It's much tougher to search for truth and think about positive things. Most people think about negative things. How do we know? Simple. Most of what comes out of people's mouths is negative. Let's face it; most of what has come out of my mouth and your mouth in the past has been negative as well.

You can change that! It's a choice. I made the change—you can, too.

Do you want to succeed? Be positive. Get rid of fear and prejudice and work at thinking and speaking good and positive things. Don't be so quick to prejudge others and situations. To prejudge is the easy and lazy way out.

Let's be stronger than that. Let's think and speak about things that encourage and bring out a fresh perspective. Let's speak creative ideas when everyone else is speaking with anger or just whining or complaining. That's the shine! You can shine; you can succeed even more.

Life applications

Keep practicing and working at these concepts of thinking and speaking positively, and shine on you will. But remember: It takes effort every minute of every day to pay attention to every thought that is going in and out of your head. But stay with it, and soon your whole perspective will change. And believe me, others will notice and like the change. More importantly, you will notice and begin to enjoy the good things that come out of your mouth as a result of the good things that you are thinking in your mind.

Journal entry 2

Are there things in your life that you can now see as prejudice? Where did those lies come from? What can you do to change those prejudices now?

Clearing the Clutter – SECTION 3

LESSON 2

Quick thought

When we prejudge people, we allow fear and anger to separate us from others for really no reason. In fact, a lot of prejudice is really junk floating around our minds that came from other people, and we foolishly chose to believe it

It's time to kick those things out and find out what you have been missing. Check out my story. This really happened to me, and it will help you better understand what we miss out on when we allow the lies of prejudice to separate us from others.

Storytime

"The Harley Hogs of Amish Country"

In conclusion

Again, like everything else, the answer to prejudice is honor. We don't have to respect and agree with every group or individual; however, we can still honor every person and group by realizing that just like us, they have the freedom to make their own choices. We simply need to allow them to do that.

Honor does not allow a bunch of lies and bad feelings to separate us. Just like the bikers I came face to face with. Would I hang out with them? Would they want me to tag along on their next journey? Probably not, however, all us enjoyed that moment together.

In the case of racial and cultural differences, we don't have to like everything about others either. But we can still appreciate the differences instead of foolishly being angry and fearful.

Prejudice reminds me of my neighbor's twin dogs. They bark all the time, and I get really tired of it. Sometimes I mumble to myself, "Stupid mutts." Recently, someone told me that dogs bark when they're afraid and when they don't understand something. Like I said, "Stupid mutts!" It kind of reminds me of what all of us are like when we choose to act out of prejudice. We are simply standing in the front yard barking our heads off out of fear and stupidity.

Well, since dogs can be trained to stop barking at every little thing, certainly we can stop, too. And just as those dogs now can spend their time chasing butterflies and chewing on their little doggy biscuits, we, too, can use our time thinking and doing positive and productive things instead of wasting our valuable time and energy on prejudice.

LA4 – Prejudice is to Prejudge

the Harley Hogs of Amish Country

It was summertime, and I was 16. I had been detasseling corn for the fourth summer in a row, and I'd managed to save a little money. Most of my friends were buying cars, but I didn't have enough cash, so I decided to get a little motorcycle instead. Besides, I didn't really need a car since the family Country Squire LTD station wagon, complete with side wood paneling, was at my disposal . . . and boy, what a great sound system! I could really jam to my 8-track of "The Bee Gees Live."

I bought a little Kawasaki that was good both on the road and off. From that time on, I was riding the trails with friends or exploring in serene solitude my new frontier: the forgotten farms of Amish country. While on one of these expeditions, I had an experience I'll never forget.

It was a soft summer Saturday, and I was rolling along at a modest 20 to 30 mph. With one hand gently adjusting the throttle, and the other planted on my knee, I looked to and fro, enjoying the beauty of all creation and the simple serenity of hand-tied bales drying in the hay fields. Suddenly, the scene was shattered as the breeze brought the menacing sounds of man's machinery, jolting me back to reality.

Peering down the road, I saw a bold parade of 30 to 40 Harley Davidsons cruising my way. The riders wore long hair and black leather vests; on their bare biceps they sported tattoos, probably mentioning "Mother." They looked as out of place in this "land that time forgot" as an Amish buggy would look rolling along a Los Angeles freeway at rush hour.

As the "hogs" rumbled toward me, fear entered my heart, and my mind began looking for an escape. Not only were they bearing down on me, they were covering the entire road. I was doomed. I practically closed my eyes, bracing myself. But wait . . . what was this? Slowly at first, then as if by choreography, the bikers began peeling off to make room for this skinny kid on a dirt bike. When I passed the first group of riders, my fear transformed to excitement. With fist clenched and elbow firm, I gave them the bikers' salute. As I continued on, one by one and two by two the leather-clad men returned my salute, sometimes with a slight smile.

Sure, I'm still embarrassed by my reaction of fear and prejudice. I had looked for a way out but couldn't find it. As a result, I experienced a thrill I remember to this day. I can't help but wonder how many times my fear and prejudices have kept me from the exhilaration of a shared moment with another human being, who appears to be very different from me, even though we're really a lot alike.

Well, I guess I'll never know. But, for a moment in time, "me and the boys" were brothers.

Troy

SECTION 3

The Problem with PRIDE

LESSON 1

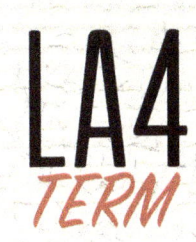

LA4 TERM: To be prideful or proud simply means to be unteachable. It's the false notion that somehow you are better or more important than someone else, that somehow you have "already arrived" or that you've "got it all together."

The problem with pride (and this is not to be confused with the pride of a job well done) is that it inhibits us from admitting that a mistake has been made. On the contrary: Everyone makes mistakes.

Pride also keeps one from looking at faults and addressing those issues. As you have been learning in LA4, we need to always change and improve. These are what bring humility and success.

Pride promotes cover-ups—in other words, the prideful will often lie to cover up the reality of their mistake or wrongdoing. It often keeps people from trying again after a mistake. As mentioned before, the humble know that mistakes are useful and show what works and what doesn't.

Quick thought

The worst part of pride is that it keeps people right where they are because they aren't teachable. As a result, pride keeps us from our goal of doing our best, working hard and honoring those in authority.

LA4 – The Problem with Pride

Ironically, the prideful always think they should be in authority, but those who walk in pride are anything but leaders.

Sure, you have been doing well. You have learned to honor and learned about humility. You have been learning to take an honest look at your faults and then have begun the process of changing. That's great! However, pride is something we all must guard against every day.

It can sneak up on us at any time and ruin all that we have worked for. Or, as in the story you are about to read, sometimes pride simply leads to an embarrassing situation.

Storytime

"You Wouldn't Dare"

Discussion questions

Please describe a time or two when, like Doug, you got a little proud and paid the price. (For anyone at this point who says, "I've not paid the price like that for pride," a bigger price for pride is more than likely on the horizon.)

_____
_____
_____
_____
_____
_____

What could Doug have done to avoid the milk bath, and what could you have done differently in your situation that would have kept you from a similar fate?

_____
_____
_____
_____
_____

'You Wouldn't Dare'

It was my junior year at Taylor University when I witnessed a scene of what might be termed unwarranted daring. I remember the situation well. It started when my roommate and I left our third-floor dorm room and headed toward the Dining Commons for lunch. It was May, and the last week of finals had begun.

This trip was slightly different from our usual noontime ritual, as Dave was carrying our one-gallon pitcher in hopes of obtaining a free fill-up of milk. If there's one thing a college student needs during finals, in addition to pizza, it's plenty of milk and coffee. The beverages simply had to be there to wash down the enormous quantities of Oreos and Chips Ahoy cookies being consumed all night long—a college student's soul food, especially when the studying was constant.

After a quick lunch, Dave and I enjoyed a "one time only" complimentary gallon of milk. The cooks told us this with a smile because we had been the only ones to approach them. However, it came with a warning, "Don't ask again."

Heading for our room, we were feeling free, the sun reminding us that summer was but a week away. We quickly wove through the traffic of would-be lunchers and, having filled the pitcher to the brim, the other students happily made room. There were smiles and yells of delight: "Whoa!" "What do you guys got there?" and "Hey, wait a second, I'll get my cup." Others simply laughed and commented to friends.

Soon we were heading up the stairs toward our room, moving quickly but carefully, not wanting to spill a precious drop. As we opened the door to the third floor, Doug Samson was on his way out, and we almost collided. We all started to laugh as we realized the potential of what almost happened.

And it would have been especially costly for Doug, a friend, but not a close one. He always wore the trendiest outfits, and this day was no different for "Dapper Doug." Golf shirt, stylish Bermuda shorts, white tennis shoes.

Well, after a quick chuckle, we were all about to head on our way when Dave, standing directly in front of Doug, tilted the pitcher toward him jokingly as if he were going to dump it on him. Doug's laughter and jovial smile transformed to a stiff upper lip and protruded chest. This caught Dave and me off guard. Then Doug went a step further and sternly warned, "You wouldn't dare!"

LA4 – The Problem with Pride

Dave rotated slightly toward his right, still with a puzzled look on his face, but he seemed to be asking me for final approval to do what we both now knew must happen. I just covered my face with my hand. This motion seemed to be the trigger. Dave rotated back toward Doug and, in one single motion of force, heaved the entire gallon of milk on him.

It splashed with fury against Doug's chest and chin. And as the cold liquid hit him, he didn't even move. He stood there quietly for a second, looking himself over. Then in disbelief he began to repeat, "He did it. I can't believe he did it."

Slowly, Doug turned toward the hallway and began to walk—with stiff legs now that the milk was making its way into his pin-striped Bermudas. As he disappeared down the hall, his refrain continued: "I can't believe he did it."

As Dave and I sat in our dorm room pondering the loss of our beloved liquid, we both agreed that Doug needed the milk more than we did, and we were all too willing to make the sacrifice.

Doug made a choice to rise up in pride, and he paid the price. I think of the times I myself have paraded in pride, and someone had to "rain" on me. It may not have been milk, but it still wasn't a pretty sight. But I think we all need that from time to time in order to remind us that everyone is just human. We're all frail. And no one is better than anyone else.

You've heard it said that pride comes before a fall. It's true! But we have an opportunity to change and not have to face the fall. All we have to do is humble ourselves, or a pitcher of milk just may be the "refresher" to keep us on course.

Troy

SECTION 3

Bitter or BETTER
LESSON 1

Journal entry

Take a look at yourself and see if there are areas of pride that you walk in every day. (Remember, all of us have areas of pride we need to remove. So, if you don't see anything, that's a problem in itself. If you need to, ask a friend or co-worker; they can tell you.) Maybe it's a bad attitude regarding a specific responsibility at work or maybe it's something you do when you're around a specific group. Either way, describe the problem and how it relates to pride. Devise a plan to begin changing now before you pay a price (like Doug from the story) or before it inhibits your success.

> **LA4 TERM** There are three more destructive behaviors or thought patters that need to be removed before we can head into the final section where everything comes together and you learn to fly a lot higher.

They are unforgiving, bitterness and envy (envy will be discussed in the next lesson). An example of unforgiving may be witnessed every day as a friend at work is mad at someone else. As a result, your friend makes a statement that he or she will not forgive the other person, then hold on to that all day long. At the end of the day, your friend is an angry mess while the other person who chose to go on with life may not even remember the situation.

LA4 – Bitter or Better

The problem with unforgiving is that it's like any other bad decision; it becomes a pattern if it isn't dealt with. In other words, if your friend doesn't forgive this time, he or she may choose not to forgive next time in a similar situation, and each time it gets easier and easier not to forgive. Over a period of time, that person is often nasty, even when nobody has done anything wrong to him or her. That is bitterness.

Think of when something tastes bitter and how your face looks when you taste it. It's no different with bitterness that comes after someone chooses not to forgive. Eventually, it's right there on his face for all to see. And just as when something tastes bitter you spit it out of your mouth, so it is with those who are full of bitterness. You want to get away as fast as you can. Don't let this happen to you. Forgive others.

There are many other consequences from bitterness. For example, some collegiate studies suggest that a number of physical ailments, including some chronic illnesses, can be the result of long-term bitterness. One study even defined bitterness as "unforgiveness." And it's important to note that was in a non-religious study.

Bitterness can happen to any of us simply by not forgiving others and going on with life. You see, forgiving others when they do something bad to us is more for our benefit than theirs. The best part? With forgiveness comes freedom.

As we have previously discussed, we cannot control, nor should we try to control, what others do, but we can do the right thing: forgive and move on. That brings joy, success and prosperity. If others want to hold onto the past, that's their problem. But you know better. Toss it off your back and ride on!

Journal entry 2

Is there anyone whom you need to forgive? More than likely there is. Simply write down their name and a little about the situation; and then write something like this: "I choose to forgive (name) and forget the situation. I am not perfect, and I have hurt others, too. I hope for his sake that he forgives me as well. My future is too big and too bright to be held back by an unforgiving attitude."

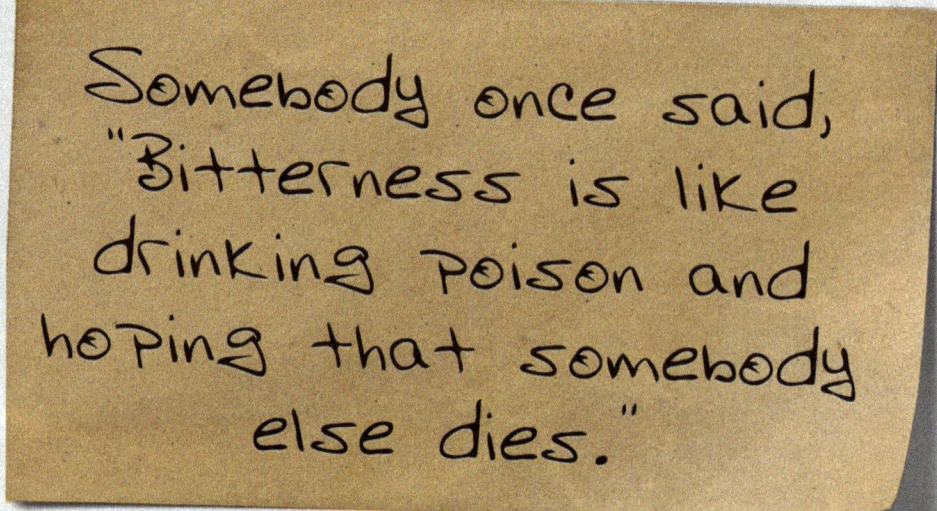

Somebody once said, "Bitterness is like drinking poison and hoping that somebody else dies."

SECTION 3

Envy is YOUR ENEMY

LESSON 1

LA4 TERM

Envy is wishing you had something that is not rightfully yours. Envy, like prejudice, can lead to anger, rage and serious acts of violence.

Quick thought

The bottom line to envy is that many people aren't happy with themselves or what they have, so they become envious of others' possessions or situations. For example: new car, big house or good job.

Lazy people sit and complain about what they don't have. Those with a future work hard and honor others.

There's an answer to envy. It's easy: Work hard, honor others and forget about what others have. You haven't walked in their shoes, and you have no idea how their life really is—even if they "have it made." So what? Be happy for them. Maybe they worked harder than most or risked much to get what they have. That alone deserves your honor.

LA4 – Envy is Your Enemy

Somebody is always going to have more money, be better looking or have an easier way to go. That's the way it is. Until we deal with that, we can never realize our own full potential. That's all we can do—do our best and look for opportunities to change and grow. That, my friends, is a productive and prosperous life.

Both the joy and thrill of life are in the challenge—the challenge of developing the skills and talents each of us has been given. That's what LA4 is all about—to help you position yourself to succeed, getting rid of envy, unforgiving attitudes and bitterness.

Discussion questions

Recount at least one true-life story of someone you may have been envious of—like a famous athlete, musician or movie star—only to find out later that he or she has serious emotional problems; has broken the law on several occasions; or has injured himself, herself or others. (Obviously, things are not always as they appear.)

_____
_____
_____
_____
_____
_____

List a few things that others have (you don't need to name the individual) that you are at least a little envious of.

_____
_____
_____
_____
_____
_____
_____

Clearing the Clutter – SECTION 3

Can you live without those things?

_____
_____
_____
_____
_____
_____
_____

Are you strong enough to put all that aside and use that energy and desire to work hard at honoring and improving your talents? Devise a strategy of what to do next time the envious feeling hits.

_____
_____
_____
_____
_____
_____
_____

Discuss one positive thing that all the time spent envying others has done for you. Zero! Exactly!

_____
_____
_____
_____
_____
_____
_____

Section 3: Summary

LESSON 1

Quick thought

It all comes down to guarding your mind against junk. You have to see the junk for what it is. Lies that harm your future are your only real enemy—lies that say you're no good, lies that say you're better than others, lies that would have you hold a grudge or not forgive, and lies that judge others by their appearance. That's the stuff that hinders opportunity, not only for the future but every day as well. Kick that stuff out before it does any more harm, focus on the positive and walk on.

Remember, this section is like everything else we have done in LA4: I It must be practiced every single day, or you will go directly back to the old ways that lead to failure. You're not a failure! You have come this far, and you're stronger and more humble than when we started this together. You're stronger because you understand more truth, and you are learning to honor in a deeper way. You're more humble because you realize that everybody makes mistakes. You also realize that everyone has choices to make and, even if they're the wrong ones, each person has the right to make those decisions without being hassled, hammered or controlled by others. That means you and me, too!

You can't force people to do the right thing. If they're teachable, you may speak the truth to them. Then allow them the freedom to make their own decision and move on. That's honor.

SUMMARY OF SECTION

Why is it important to pay attention to your thoughts?

_____
_____
_____
_____
_____

SECTION 3

What differences are you seeing in your life as a result of changing those negative thoughts to positive thoughts? Also, are others noticing yet?

_____
_____
_____
_____
_____

Why does fear lead to failure?

_____
_____
_____
_____
_____
_____
_____

LESSON 2

SUMMARY OF SECTION

Discuss strategies for avoiding bitterness.

_____
_____
_____
_____
_____
_____
_____

LA4 - Summary

Why must we forgive and forget?

_____
_____
_____
_____
_____
_____
_____
_____
_____

What does it accomplish to be envious of others? So, what's the answer to removing the poison of envy from your life? In other words, what should you do instead of being envious?

_____
_____
_____
_____
_____
_____
_____
_____

Clearing the Clutter - SECTION 3

SPECIAL NOTE

If you are going to succeed, you simply must avoid bitterness at all costs. Any bad thing that happens at all, immediately your response should be something like this: "I choose to forgive (name)." Say it in your mind or even out loud: "My future is too big and too bright to let this interfere in any way."

I don't care if it's wintertime; force open that window and shout it out if you have to. This is big! Do what you must to get rid of it. You've come a long way—let's keep going.

Journal entry

Describe some thought patterns that you have changed. Be specific as to negative thoughts that you were entertaining—and now have replaced with positive thoughts.

Also, describe the surprising amount of effort it takes to change those bad thoughts to good thoughts.

If you are strong enough, rededicate yourself to continuing in the process of improving your thought life from negative, destructive thoughts to positive, fresh and creative thoughts that honor others and consider their situation above your own.

Establishing Hope and Vision

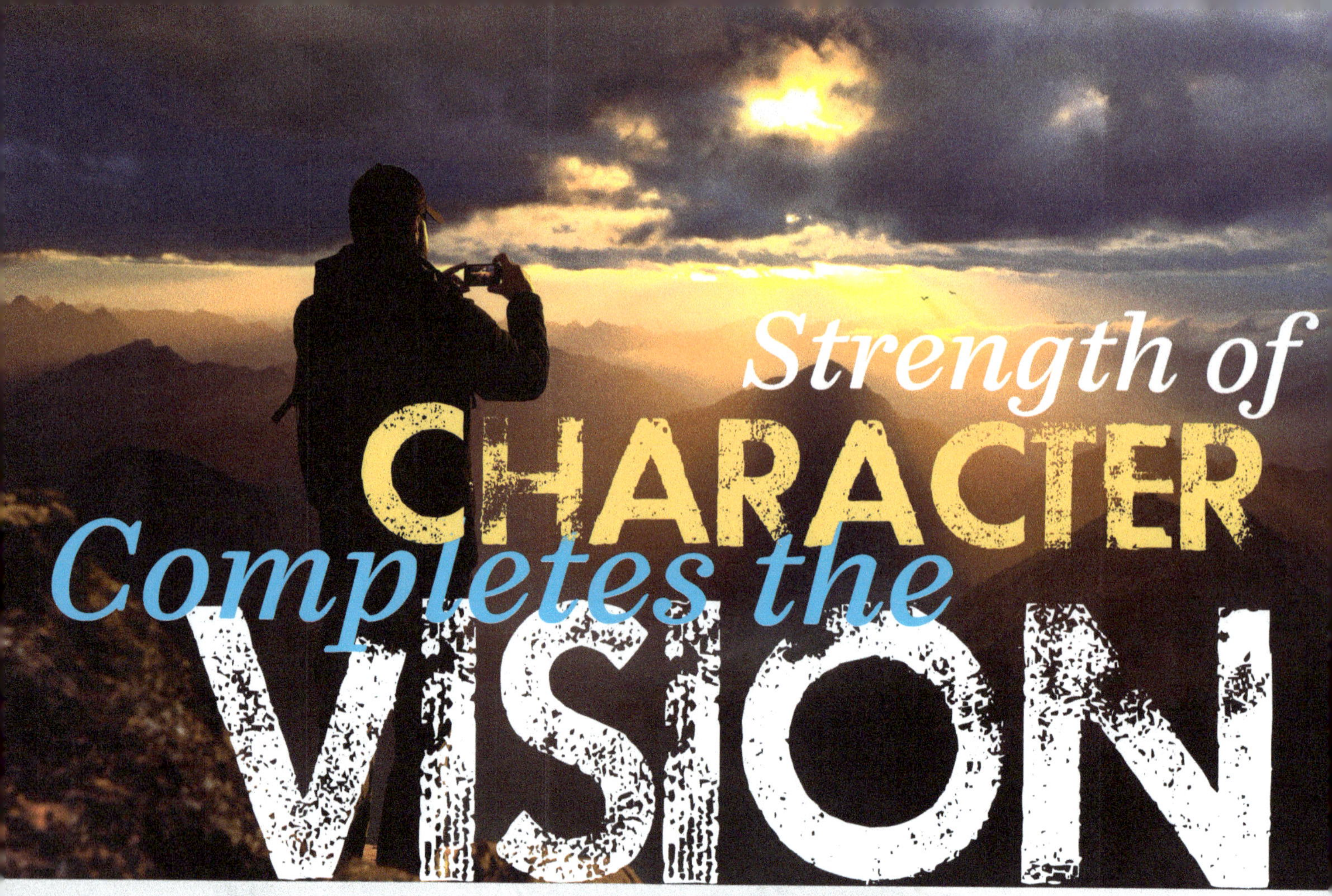

Strength of CHARACTER Completes the VISION

LESSON 1

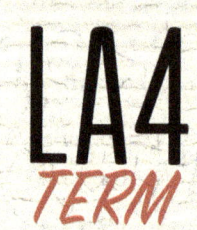

LA4 TERM

Again, character is doing the right thing at the right time (Section 2). It's a personal constitution or contract of what you stand for. That includes lines that you will not cross. People of strong character have a healthy respect for law and order.

As a person of strong character, you understand that laws are neither for you nor against you. They are there to bring order.

Always remember, to fully be strong in character and honor, you must live, love and speak truth. You will not be right all the time, but if you look for truth, you will find it most of the time, and strength and success are yours.

© 2000 - 22 TROY... Pure Blue Creative, LLC LA4™

Quick thought

Think about it—when you had a strong boss or teacher or parent who laid down the law, then backed it up with authority, peace and order reigned. This is true especially when you know that it's out of honor and respect that those rules are there. That is strong character and leadership.

Activity

Send at least three separate notes to individuals who practice the leadership and character qualities mentioned above. These notes could be sent to a boss, a parent, former teacher or other person in authority. Even if you don't agree with everything that these leaders do or did, that's OK. You can still make mention of the qualities that you see in them. You will be amazed how much of an encouragement your letters will be to these leaders.

Also, make sure your letters are neatly and well written. Anything written in excellence contributes positively to your message.

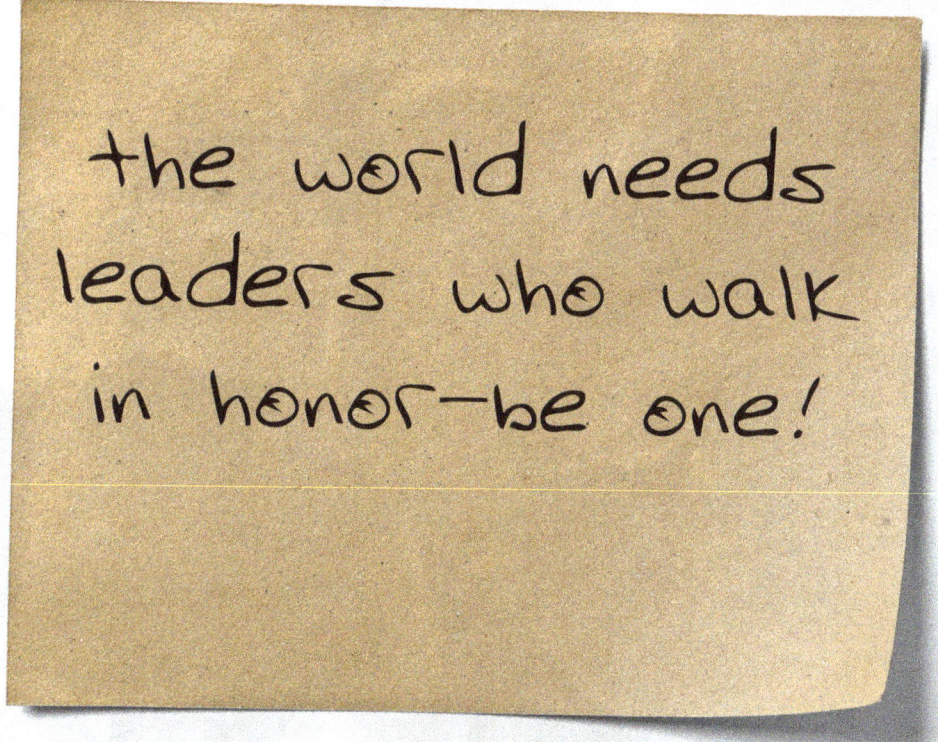

Gotta have VISION

LESSON 1

Quick thought

We have been through many concepts of honor, truth, guarding what goes into our minds and much more. Now it's time to put it all together.

The idea is for you not only to work toward a successful future but to begin prospering and living a successful life now at an even greater measure.

> **LA4 TERM** — Vision is the "big picture." It's the dream. It should be based on your present skills and the development of future skills.

Also, if there is no vision or focus as to where you are going, life becomes meaningless, bitterness sets in, anger and laziness dominate your days. But there is a better plan for you. In fact, you have already begun the new life of liberty and purpose by joining me in LA4. You are beginning to see the type of person that you can be and that you want to be. That is vision.

© 2000 - 22 TROY... Pure Blue Creative, LLC LA4™

Establishing Hope and Vision – SECTION 4

You are not limited to one vision. There are personal visions, which is what we were just talking about. There are professional visions—that is what you hope and dream as your business life continues to develop. And the list can go on and on.

We reach our vision by setting goals. Goals can be long-term or short-term. Goals keep us on track for the vision. Without achieving goals, you will never reach your vision. For example: "I enjoy working with my hands; I would like to be a carpenter, maybe a mechanic," or "I want to own a business someday," or even "I would like to work with computers in my future job."

That is as far as most people get. Very few ever end up in the occupation that they would have enjoyed the most because they failed to make it a clear vision and set goals NOW! However, it can be different with you. You are heading down the road of success, and each goal you accomplish is one giant step closer to your destination—your vision.

Journal entry

The purpose of this journal assignment is to help you see that no matter what you do, whether small or great, it takes vision and accomplishing goals to get there. Please give a couple of examples from your own life of how you have had a vision, set goals and ultimately accomplished your final goals, thus achieving your vision.

It could be what you did back in high school to prepare for tryouts of an athletic team, music, drama or any other club at school. Maybe it was a project for a class assignment, and you had to build something. You first had a vision of what you wanted to build, then you set goals like buying the material, putting various sections together, maybe painting it a specific color and guess what? There it was. Your vision was completed. Perhaps then you chose an interest to pursue a college degree. You accomplished that and now you're in the profession of your choice but you have goals to grow in your career … vision is all about the little victories along the way that create momentum and confidence to dream bigger and reach higher. Celebrate every victory. Go back over your accomplishments no matter how long ago or how small—whatever it takes to keep the fire burning.

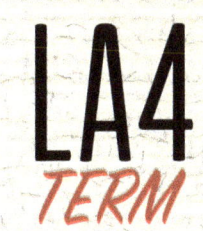

LA4 TERM — Although we discussed goals in the previous lesson, it's important to clarify both short-term and long-term goals. Short-term goals could mean a week to several months. A long-term goal would obviously be more in the future—for example, one, two or even five years down the road.

Without staying on track your goals will never be achieved.

LA4 – Gotta Have Vision

Quick thought

Don't worry; your vision for the future may change as you develop new interests and skills. You simply need to adjust your goals so that they're achievable—and so they keep you on track with your new vision.

Changing your vision and goals frequently shows an obvious sign of discontentment, confusion and maybe even laziness, since it's easy to float and say, "Oh, I thought I wanted to do this, but now I'm not so sure. Maybe I'll try something else instead." That kind of pattern obviously leads nowhere.

Remember, it's OK to change course a bit, but keep going forward. Keep setting goals and reaching them. The great thing about goals is that as you reach each one, your confidence grows and grows. You get stronger, your vision gets clearer and your future gets brighter and brighter

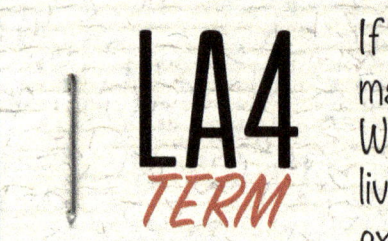

If there's one thing lacking today among many people of all ages, it's the lack of hope. What is hope? It's purpose. It's a reason for living, moving and growing. It is ultimately an expectation of success.

Now that you have come this far with LA4, you are learning to expect success. Hope is building within you as you continue to improve those skills related to humility and honor. Add that to your new understanding of vision and goals; and you are ready to shine.

As your hope and vision grow, you'll find that you get out of bed that much quicker and easier. People will want to be around you because you're happy, you're positive and you have purpose. Life is great for those on the move.

Journal entry

As we prepare for what's coming in these final lessons, now is a good time to look at your vision. Discuss the vision you have for yourself. Maybe it's a personal vision of the type of person you want to be. Also, include your vision of a future job, maybe an advance of where you are now or a completely different career, and family. Don't be afraid to write how you really feel about these issues. There is nothing to be ashamed of. This is your future. I'm for you!

Take some time to really write this from the heart. When you're finished, maybe you can share it with a family member or a friend you can really trust. But guard it. Don't just trust anyone with it.

Establishing Hope and Vision – SECTION 4

Life applications

Begin looking for someone who has a noble purpose—a vision that focuses on the benefit of others—then begin helping that person in any way possible. As always, continue to honor all authority figures, and your vision will get clearer as your future continues to get brighter.

LESSON 2

Quick thought

As you labor with others and honor their vision, certainly your vision will further develop, too. As it does, don't be afraid to dream bigger and reach higher. It is fitting for people like you to set a course that few others are able to take because you have learned to honor others, work hard and change. Now comes the payoff!

Interestingly enough, to really dream big, we need to have the faith of a child. We need to go back to those days when we weren't afraid to think big—when we weren't ashamed of the passion and potential that we saw in ourselves.

Check out my story.

Storytime

"The Bow-tie Drummer Boy"

> **SPECIAL NOTE**
>
> So, let's dream like children. Let's set our sights higher and higher as we go. But remember that, even in the story, I not only set a vision, I practiced every day for months. Even if most people dare to dream big, few are dedicated enough to work at it every single day. You are.
>
> You've been learning honor and learning to labor in it every day. You're ready to develop a vision, set goals and begin to succeed at a whole new level. Let's go with the strength and maturity of honor...and the faith of a child. The world is in desperate need of you.

LA4 – Gotta Have Vision

the Bow-tie Drummer Boy

I don't remember well the year I was four years old, but I do recollect longing for a drum set. I had seen someone play the drums on television, and I had decided that I'd like to do the same.

The drummer's arms whipped recklessly around the many drum heads, and the sound made my heart thump along with each beat. I knew, if given the chance, I could move like that and make music. Plus, as a preschooler, if there was one thing I loved, it was pounding on things – anything.

By the time Christmas morning rolled around, I may have mentioned my desired gift a few times – a few thousand times. It was one of the things that I never really expected to get, but I did. I got the drums.

My parents, staying with the musical theme, bought my 5-year-old brother a trumpet he didn't ask for. He seemed happy, though, so I didn't have the heart to tell him what I was thinking: I got the better end of the deal. I could bang, clang, crash and sing – yes, sing. I know drums are not traditionally used for singing, but that's how they made me feel. And so I sang.

After their "little drummer boy" had played throughout Christmas day, I'm sure my parents realized the folly of their decision and began hoping I would eventually lose interest or that the paper heads on the drums might have a tragic tear. Well, yes, the drum tops were paper and not all that loud; however, the cymbals were real, and my sticks found them frequently with glee.

The history of these drums gets a little foggy for me here, but my mother tells me I persisted for several months with a practicing routine. She says I would awaken early, put on my best and only blue suit, bow tie and buckle shoes, and head to the corner of the living room where my drums were allowed to live. From there I proceeded to the stereo (you know the kind: huge, wood console with giant opening door atop, and record player inside with three speeds – 33, 45 and 78.)

I would cue up the same song, probably the only record my parents owned with drums on it, and then return to my drum set and play and sing along. After the performance of the same song three or four times, I would go back to my room, change into my regular play clothes and scarcely touch the drums until the next morning.

As I look back, I'm amazed at the commitment I made to those drums. But at the age of four, I got a vision of something and set myself to it. And in my childish mind, that dream became a reality for me every day for months to come. Maybe I kept going because nobody told me how foolish I was. Or maybe someone tried, but it didn't matter because I was too young to worry about what someone else thought.

I don't know why I eventually quit playing the drums. Perhaps it was because I had already achieved that goal, and it was time to move on to something bigger and better. But as I grew older, I found that as my realities got bigger, my dreams tended to get smaller. Maybe that's happened to you as well.

It's not too late, though! We can still go back to where we left off. And it will take the faith of a child. So let's pick up those sticks and play with passion; let's rise above the opinion of others; let's commit ourselves to the vision. When that dream has been realized, we can dedicate ourselves to the next vision, and the next and even the next. For that is life — and growth and freedom.

How about it? Let's clip on our bow ties and rock-n-roll!

Troy

CAMARADERIE

LESSON 1

LA4 TERM

Camaraderie is finding those with whom you have something in common. It's finding those people of like mind and vision. It doesn't have to be the same vision, but it does need to be someone who understands vision and serving and honoring others.

If you are to continue on the path of honor and vision, it is important to find these people. There are not a lot of them out there, granted, but they're increasing in number every day, thanks to people like you.

Quick thought

Just as it's important to find people of honor, it's equally important to stay away from those who don't understand or practice honor. All they will do is ridicule you and try to bring you down to their level. People of dishonor often criticize those who are honoring and laboring for a vision. Again, the reason is that it's much easier to criticize than to work and change negative patterns.

Maybe you're familiar with the saying, "You can't soar with the eagles if you're hanging out with the turkeys." This is true. Some may say, "Oh, that's mean." It's not mean; it's reality. You are either going forward or you are going backward. There is no in-between. Others will either help build you up or knock you down. As soon as you step out and say, "This is my vision," those of dishonor will trample it to the ground. Don't give them a chance.

It's a vulnerable thing to share a vision. It can be scary.

LA4 – Camaraderie

Check out my story.

Storytime

"Big Boots, Big Heart"

Discussion questions

Have you ever experienced a quiet, gentle moment of sharing from the heart like Randy and I did?

_____
_____
_____
_____
_____

If the answer is "yes," what was the moment like? If the answer is "no," speculate as to what you may have said in a moment like that.

_____
_____
_____
_____
_____
_____
_____
_____
_____

Big Boots, Big Heart

Randy Hite was one of my childhood friends. He wasn't any taller than the rest of us third-graders, but he had a short body and unusually long legs. Randy always wore cowboy boots that sort of flopped along at the end of his rubbery legs.

Although Randy lived in Texas only until he was two, he talked with a slow drawl like his daddy. His father was his hero, which made it unspeakably sad when he was killed that year, having fallen from atop a silo at work.

Randy missed only a few days of school, but it took several months before we really began to relate again. I remember when Randy surprised the whole gang with an invitation to a slumber party at his house. About 10 of us rode the bus home with him on a Friday night.

We had pizza and ice cream; we played kickball and tag. What a night. I remember his mom as well. She was much too pretty, we thought, to be the mother of someone we knew. It turns out she was understanding, too, as we would soon discover.

As Calpurnia says about some young boys in the novel To Kill a Mockingbird, we got the "look arounds" about 1 a.m. and, from Randy's top bunk bed, climbed through his bedroom window into the darkness of the night. We quickly got caught in a rainstorm and scrambled back in the window as fast as we could.

With six or seven wiggling, squirrelly third-graders on top of the bed, it gave way and crashed with a loud thud, breaking into several pieces. Randy's mother rushed in, and there we were: wet little boys sitting on a busted bed. We braced ourselves for the worst, only to hear, "You boys better get some towels."

As third grade came to a close, I had spent the night at Randy's several times—just the two of us. We had become great friends. Randy always had been a gentle soul. But since his father's death, he had a humility, a wisdom, that went beyond his 10 years. Yet he still managed to maintain the freshness of childhood.

I'll never forget the last night we would hang out together before Randy and his mom moved back to Texas to be near family. We were up even later than usual into the wee hours of the morning.

I was pecking away at a little red typewriter that Randy had, and he was drawing pictures of badges—a badge that he would one day wear with

LA4 – Camaraderie

pride. Randy wanted to be a firefighter. He wanted to help people. And in the dark hours he dug down deep and said, "Maybe I can save someone like my dad. Someone who got caught in a jam."

After a moment of silence, Randy's comment gave me the courage to share what others would only laugh at in the daylight: "I want to be a writer. I want to write stuff that makes a difference."

Randy didn't say anything. He only nodded quietly, and I felt it was okay. These were the nights, with adults safely in bed, that we loved as children, because no one was around to douse the fires of our dreams with the cold water of their reality.

I believe that Randy's reality is just what he said it would be: He's down there in Texas fighting fires and saving folks who are "in a jam."

Thank God for faithful souls like Randy, who aren't afraid to search their hearts to find their calling—and still have the grace to encourage others to do the same.

Troy

Establishing Hope and Vision – SECTION 4

LESSON 2

Discussion questions

Have you ever had a friend like Randy? Do you now? If so, what is (was) he or she like?

_____
_____
_____
_____

What is the value of having a friend like Randy who desires to help others and has the strength to share his vision without shame?

_____
_____
_____
_____
_____

Just as you long to have a friend like Randy, are you one? Please explain areas where you feel you are a good friend, and maybe share some areas of friendship that need improvement.

_____
_____
_____
_____
_____

Can you think of some of your current "friends" who are not people of honor and vision? If so, are you strong enough to spend less time with those people and more time with friends of like mind and vision?

_____
_____
_____

LA4 – Camaraderie

Quick thought

As mentioned earlier, it may sound kind of mean to walk away from some of your current friends; however, if they are not going forward, they are certainly going backward, and if you continue to spend much of your time with people like that, you won't move on. They will hold you back.

As you begin to honor more and more, this concept of finding friends of like mind and vision will be easy because after you begin to walk in honor, you will not want dishonor around you. There is no reason to feel guilty either. If they choose to honor, they are more than welcome to come along—if not, SEE YA. I'm movin' on.

Journal entry

Reflect on some individuals or a group of friends who presently have no desire to walk in honor and vision. Then prepare a course of action to move toward those of honor. The reason you need a plan is simply because as you leave this other group you are going to hear all kinds of criticism. You don't turn and criticize them, you simply state that you are heading in a different direction. Then do it quickly and move on. That takes strength. If you don't make the break, you'll be right back in the old junk in no time.

SECTION 4

HONOR
Brings Relationship

LESSON 1

LA4 TERM

Relationship is quality interaction between human beings. It is also a working together for the good of both (Teamwork; Section 1 and Camaraderie; Section 4). There cannot be any true form of relationship without trust. Trust comes from consistent honor.

If you are a person of honor, you will have quality relationships. Relationships that bring joy and fulfillment to both you and the other person. With honor, relationships can develop and prosper because each person involved is concerned about the well-being of the other.

Quick thought

Honor in relationship is, unfortunately, not a common thing these days. Take a look around you, and it will become clear that many relationships are based on selfishness. In other words, each person is trying to control and get what he or she wants. As a result, there is a constant tug and pull between the two people. Neither person will ever be content with that type of relationship, even the one who gets his or her way most of the time.

As we discussed before, for those who operate out of dishonor and control, they will never be satisfied. They will always want more and, even if they continue to get their way, in the end they will be bitter. Only honor brings contentment, fulfillment and success. All those things are yours as you continue to honor others.

LA4 – Camaraderie

Just as we learned about camaraderie in the previous lesson with my ol' buddy Randy, check out the Carpenter family and learn more about honor in relationships.

Storytime

"Barefoot on a Banana"

Discussion questions

Ron obviously said something he shouldn't have about Mrs. Hughes; however, he got away with it because of the honor in that relationship up to that point. Recall some situations where you made a mistake in a relationship and it was OK because there had been honor there. And recall a time where you did not get away with a similar mistake because there had not been a lot of honor—it was just one more bad thing, and that person finally had enough.

The entire Carpenter family enjoyed serving others. Do you know some people like this? What are they like?

_____
_____
_____
_____
_____
_____

Are you seeing even more clearly how people will feel about you as you continue to honor them? Please explain.

_____
_____
_____
_____
_____
_____
_____
_____

Barefoot on a Banana

I met the twins, Ron and Richard Carpenter, in fifth grade just after I moved to the small farm town of Millersburg, Indiana. As I had many new friends to meet, I didn't really notice them that much until Ron got his leg caught in an auger at the family-owned grain mill.

I remember seeing a picture of Ron in the paper and reading a quote from him saying "thank you" after the firefighters rescued him.

A few months later, Ron returned to school with a wooden leg and received the compassion of his classmates. But it wasn't long before Ron's fun-loving personality won the hearts of his fellow students, and the grace of our compassion was no longer needed. Ron was one of us again.

By the time junior high rolled around, my parents had switched churches, and I was attending the same one as "the boys," as I had begun to call them. I got to know them better as we now did things together at both school and church.

Ron had a quick wit and a good set shot, and Richard would smile from ear to ear, reminiscent of Milton Berle. Richard also liked girls. Not in a provocative sense, but in appreciation. He would watch them and joke with them. He had a gentleness about him that would be even more rare these days, and the girls seemed to enjoy him. But Richard was shy and graduated from high school without ever asking a girl on a date.

At church, Mr. Carpenter, the boys' dad, was our Sunday school teacher. He was older than my parents, yet full of life. He was a parental prankster who would tease the girls and hassle the guys, and we all loved it. The church parties at the Carpenters' place were like no other. There were hayrides at their farm, and in the barn we would walk barefoot in the dark, stepping on items that we were told were edible. Have you ever stepped on a banana in your bare feet?

Mrs. Carpenter was one for details, and she loved to serve others. I remember dinner at their place one evening. She stood in the kitchen, apron tied around her waist, with sleeves rolled up, refusing to eat until everyone else was happily fed. I don't know of a time when I was visiting that some form of goodies wasn't baking in her oven.

The boys' older sister, Deb, was an attractive young lady and, like her mother, an outstanding cook. Deb had spunk, and we liked to see her temper flare. We would hide her stuff and call her to the phone when nobody was there — anything to get her goat. Most of our pranks worked, but all in all, I think she probably enjoyed some of them too.

LA4 – Camaraderie

I spent more and more time with the Carpenters, and the boys and I went to high school together as well. They were good students and very respectful of their elders, which makes what happened in our Accounting class even funnier.

We had a teacher named Mrs. Hughes. We liked to joke with her before and after class when we felt she would appreciate it. One day before class, Ron, Richard and I had a question and headed to her office, which was situated directly behind her classroom. After surveying the office, and finding her absent, Ron saw a large broom in the corner and quipped, "She couldn't have gone too far; her broom is still here."

Mrs. Hughes, it turned out, had been standing directly behind us and surprised us all with the comment, "So I'm a witch, am I?"

Ron's mouth dropped wide open and he turned beet red. We awkwardly walked away with no mention of it again from Mrs. Hughes, though I thought I heard her chuckling as we made our retreat. She knew Ron well enough to know that no punishment could ever accomplish what he already felt when he saw her face.

Ron went on to take more classes from Mrs. Hughes and credited her in part for his present career as an accountant. Richard went back to college 10 years after high school, I'm told, and is now preparing to answer a call to the ministry.

As I remember these special folks, I realize that their openness in both triumph and adversity was a form of humility that allowed others in.

I'm beginning to understand that there is no greater opportunity in life than relationships. I count myself truly blessed for having known the Carpenter family.

Troy

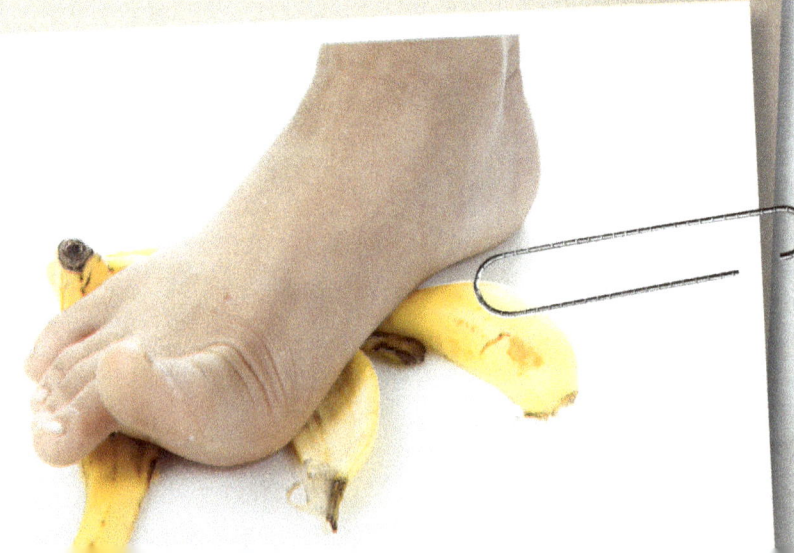

Section 4: Summary

LESSONS 1 & 2

Quick thought

Vision, achieving goals and relationship are obviously the main themes of this section; however, to be successful in these areas, you must daily recommit yourself to the material that we have covered up to this point. Vision is great but without strength of character you will never get there.

Desiring prospering relationships is good, too, but if you don't remove control and bitterness, it can't happen. Are you beginning to see how all these things that we have talked about tie together?

For now, it's important to take a concluding look at the Section 4 material. For the most benefit from this summary, please go back to the actual material and get your answers. The idea is not to see if you remember all of it, but to just reinforce the material so you better understand it and can put it into practice.

SUMMARY OF SECTION

What is vision?

_____

_____

_____

What is the importance of goals?

_____

_____

_____

_____

LA4 - Summary

Why must we have strength of character if we are to achieve goals and vision?

_____
_____
_____
_____

If you do not yet have a vision for the future, that's OK, but what is the best way to prepare and position yourself for your own vision?

_____
_____
_____
_____

What should be the No. 1 purpose in every vision?

_____
_____
_____
_____

What is the importance of camaraderie in achieving the vision?

_____
_____
_____
_____

What is the No. 1 ingredient to a successful relationship? (Big hint: the theme of LA4!)

___

Why do most people attempt to control others while in a relationship? What's wrong with that?

___

Journal entry

Please describe some relationships that you are presently involved in that need to be ended or altered. Explain why and how they must change for you to be successful in the future.

Establishing Hope and Vision – **SECTION 4**

LESSON 1

Quick thought

If you have been working hard at changing old patterns of dishonor, fear and control (to name a few) and replacing them with new patterns of honor, then expect success. Walk in it! Believe it! Life is grand for those who dare to walk in the discipline of honor—for those like you who dare to walk on the edge by developing vision and going after it with all you've got.

Yes, I said edge—as in cutting edge. As you walk in honor and vision, you will always be on the cutting edge: Very few people choose to live this way. Now you do, and I commend you. I say go and achieve your dreams, goals and visions. Go and be successful at every turn, and that means especially relationships. You are now a young man or young woman of honor, and you deserve to be treated with honor and respect.

I have waited nearly two years to write these concluding remarks to you. My desire through this whole program was and is to see you succeed. What is success? Simple. Success is the satisfaction that you have worked hard and done everything to the best of your abilities. It's achieving to your fullest potential while removing those things that are not helpful to you or others.

Martin Luther King Jr. once said, and I paraphrase: "Do your best, even if it is cleaning streets, and one day the world will beat a path to your door just to declare, 'Here is the greatest street cleaner who ever lived.'" This may be a slightly idealistic way of saying it, but Dr. King was right. A job done in honor and excellence will not go unnoticed.

In conclusion

If you think of it as you head down the road of success and prosperity, send me a card, and let me know how you are doing. I'd love to hear from you. I just know it will be great news..

Journal entry

Make a plan to keep all these life applications near at hand so that nothing is forgotten. Maybe even go through the material several times. I still do so myself.

About the Author

Troy Kidder is president of TROY … Pure Blue Creative. Kidder's public relations firm specializes in publications and digital media for communities with a readership of millions per year and growing rapidly around the country. He is a pioneer in the industry of communications, public relations and marketing for schools—serving them for over 25 years. Kidder has also done training for schools, businesses and even some Fortune 500 companies in the areas of Teamwork, Character and Creative Thinking.

A former high school English teacher, Kidder has written and published books including this character curriculum for students and adults. He is also an entrepreneur, recording artist and outstanding public speaker. Kidder's family includes his wife, their married daughter, and two little girls, and they make their home in Nashville, Tennesee.

BONUS

ANGER

LA4 TERM

Anger is an emotional response and sometimes even an explosion. It can be as subtle as a red face and the rolling of the eyes and as obvious as threats, name calling and acts of violence.

In any case, anger is always a sign of a much deeper problem. Sure, everyone gets angry at times, however, it's always appropriate to understand where that force is coming from before it turns to the severity of vulgarity or violence. Know this! The root of most anger is fear, jealousy or bitterness and sometimes even all three.

Quick thought

Often those who express anger very frequently and emphatically feel empowered as if they're "getting it off their chest." First, if they're truly getting it off their chest, why does it continue to occur? Second, someone may feel powerful for a moment, but the bottom line is that person is out of control. It's babies who throw fits until they are taught (often by some form of discipline) that screaming is not the way to get things done and that those around them just won't put up with it for long.

Ironically, it's often angry people who think they are the strong and the brave. However, these outbursts of verbal assault or physical violence are no longer just a nuisance (as in the case of a childlike tantrum) they are just plain cowardice.

It's the courageous who control their tongue and garner their actions. It's the brave who face the reality of their root issue and go after it until it is understood and finally rooted out. That's the way to prosper!

And remember, for those who continue in their anger, some form of punishment is on the way either by the law (for we live in a lawful society) or from another person more violent than they. No matter how tough someone thinks he is, there's always someone else tougher.

LA4 - Bonus

Life application

The first challenge is to use that force, that energy that comes with anger, for something positive: run, lift weights, clean out the garage or reorganize your room. If you're artistic, you can take photos, draw pictures or even build something with your hands—just get busy. By the time you get done, you may not even remember what it was that made you so angry.

Second, begin to dig into the root of that anger. Study the other chapters on fear, jealousy and bitterness. Find out if there's something someone did to you long ago that still burns inside of you and maybe that's the reason you try to punish everyone else. Forgive them. Forgive yourself. Find out what you've been afraid of and get over it. And remember, everyone has got something to deal with. It's not just you! But here's where you separate yourself from the crowd. Be courageous! Be strong! Deal with it and prosper beyond anything you've ever imagined.

LA4 TERM — A bully is someone who feels the need to hurt others to make himself feel good, significant or even powerful.

Bonus Section

When we think of the "bully" we may think back to junior high school. If only it stopped then. Strangely enough, it doesn't stop there. Maybe it's a neighbor, a relative, boss or even co-worker. One thing's for sure, no matter what age you are, they're still there. A bully is someone who feels the need to hurt others to make himself feel good, significant or even powerful. A bully often uses words and even physical violence to inflict on those he deems too weak to fight back or resist. And to go a little further, often people who feel out of control must find a way to control and/or torment others. And by definition, bullying is a pattern—not just a single act.

Quick thought

We are defined by our friends and even more so by our enemies. If you are being attacked, it's most likely because you have something (talents, beauty, brains—a future) that has stirred the contempt of an enemy. Make no mistake—the bully is an enemy trying to destroy you with words and sometimes even acts of violence. You need to see it for what it really is ... the fact is that you're on the right track, and somebody's not happy about it. Somebody's jealous. Somebody is a little intimidated. Well, isn't that just too bad.

Remember, these bull-shooters do have one skill. They not only recognize your gifts and beauty, but they can find that one area of weakness just as quickly. You've got to guard it. Again, you've got to recognize what's really going on.

Storytime

"'Stuck Up' On My Way Up"

Discussion questions

This story was not technically a case of "bullying" or "harassment," but what are some similarities to bullying that happened here?

_____

_____

_____

_____

Have you ever been misunderstood for who you are or what you are trying to accomplish?

_____

_____

_____

_____

LA4 – Bonus

Was there a way for you to clarify your intentions? If so, how did you do it and what was the response? If not, how have you handled this?

_____
_____
_____
_____
_____

Journal entry

Have you ever been accused of something that was not true when you were doing something right? What was it? How did it play out? Looking back, do you see more clearly what was going on?

Storytime

"'Jack an Eye'"

Discussion questions

How did it make you feel when I was picked on by all the camp counselors because of one thing that happened with the bully? Was that fair? Has something like that ever happened to you?

_____
_____
_____
_____
_____
_____
_____
_____

Bonus Section

How did it make you feel when the bully was told to "Jack an Eye?"

_____
_____
_____
_____
_____

I should have gone back to the coach, since he was the one in authority over the entire camp and told him what happened to me after I followed his instructions. Why do you think I was afraid to go back and tell him? Would you have gone to the coach a second time?

_____
_____
_____
_____
_____
_____
_____
_____
_____

Given the response the coach told me to tell the bully the first time, "Jack an Eye," how do you think he would have responded if he would've known I was picked on for following his instructions?

_____
_____
_____
_____
_____

LA4 - Bonus

Life applications

Whether it's verbal abuse, written cruelty or physical violence, you must expose these acts. And here's the kicker: not when the abuse is done just to you but to anyone. Don't be ashamed or afraid to talk with your superiors. I know … somebody's going to call you a "rat fink" or any other ugly name he can think of. Those are terms used by jerks who do jerky things hoping to intimidate others from shining the light on their dirty deeds. Remember, it's the foolish who sit and take it quietly from these bullies, but it's the brave who tell the truth. It's the courageous who stand up and fight for what's right. You'll be amazed how great you feel about yourself when you decide you're not going to take it.

For good leaders like this coach who is there to protect the campers and those under his authority, he can't see everything that happens at all times. He needs help from other people so he can protect those in his care. That means when we see things like this we have to speak up when things aren't right … for our sakes as well as the sake of our families and even our communities.

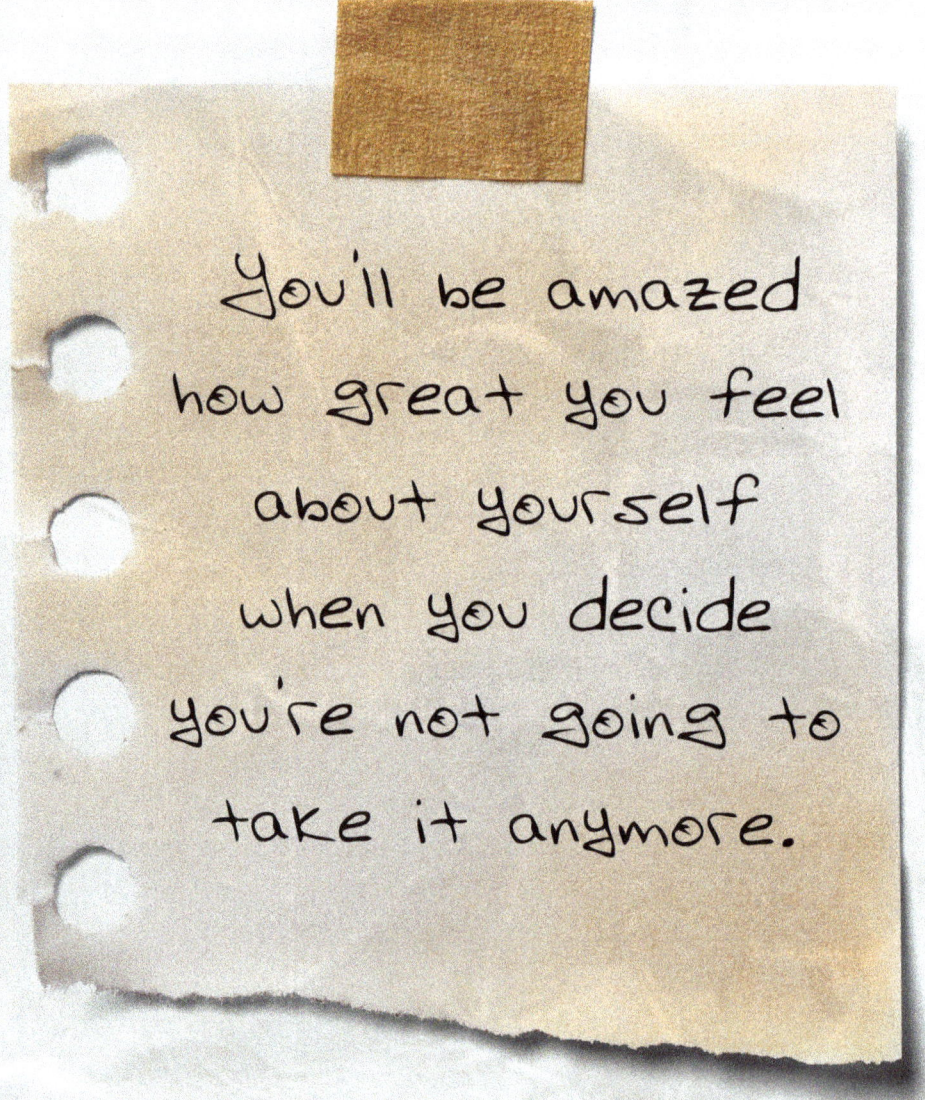

You'll be amazed how great you feel about yourself when you decide you're not going to take it anymore.

'Stuck Up' On My Way Up

Having grown up with two parents who were not only college graduates but school teachers as well, my post high school options always included some sort of university degree. However, just weeks after high school graduation a few immature summer stunts like getting laid off from work as a result of goofing off on the job, receiving a ticket for running a stop sign and occasionally staying out past curfew put my future in serious jeopardy. My dad told me that he was concerned that I didn't have what it takes to succeed in college and was considering keeping me out a year.

This scared me out of my mind. I had no other options. I resolved to change course quickly, and I did. Not only did I get my old job back, I was promoted within just a few weeks. I put aside childish behavior and just two months later, my parents were packing me off to college.

Though my dad never said it, I felt he still needed to be convinced that his middle son could make the grade at this academically sound institution. Therefore, I trotted off to college not as the victor who convinced his parents he had matured, but still a boy with even a greater challenge ahead.

The first few weeks went well. I had established a sound routine of early to bed, early to rise, and I spent nearly every night in the library. This may seem a bit extreme, but I had not been a good student in high school: I got by. I was there for the sports and the socializing, two things that I didn't concern myself with now in college, until...

...one evening my roommate Terry informed me that one of the other freshmen on our dorm wing (of about 30 other guys) made a comment about me being "Stuck up." Sure, I'd been called several names in my time, but not that one. I did some soul searching and concluded that although I had not concerned myself with friendships, I had made myself friendly: smiles and hellos on campus and in the hallways. I moved on.

A few more weeks passed as I found myself roaming down the hallway for a study break. In the distance I heard some John Denver music. I had played from his guitar songbooks for years as a child and was quite a fan so I followed the music to the open door from whence the music came. Inside the room, sitting on the floor was Steve, a fellow freshman, going through all his J.D. albums.

LA4 - Bonus

I tapped on the door and walked in. I asked if I could join him and he invited me to listen for a while. We played a few songs, chatted a bit and then I was back to the books. Terry told me the next day that Steve had been the one who made the "Stuck up" comment weeks earlier.

That night I pondered the whole thing. It just didn't make sense. I was "Stuck up" yet it was I who pursued him for relationship, not knowing his previous disposition toward me. How was I to treat him now?

That question needed no answer since Steve flunked out after the first semester. All I had known about him prior was that he attended college on an academic scholarship, something to do with a ridiculously high SAT score.

And there you have it! I wasn't "Stuck up." He was offended. Offended by my dedication to the task at hand. My force of desperation to make the grade was a flashing reminder that he could have and should have done better, certainly better than I.

Yes, somebody's always going to be smarter or more talented, but it's the hard worker, the one who gives it all he's got, who makes all the difference in this life.

So, if you're called names because of your hard work and determination, those comments are often made by those who are not willing to work as hard as you do If you're called "Stuck up," let it be on your way up.

Troy

'Jack an Eye'

Isn't it funny how things stick to the soul and don't want to let go? I was shooting some hoops the other day and for some reason my mind replayed an incident from the summer of my freshman year in high school some 25 years earlier.

I was 15 years old and had set a goal to improve in my basketball skills by practicing every day and by going away to basketball camp at a college just 30 miles away. I had exceeded all hopes the prior season by being moved up from the freshman team to play at the junior varsity level, and I even got invited to practice with the varsity squad on occasion. My sophomore year was to be my "break out" year and I just knew this week-long camp would help me develop the edge I needed.

The first two days went well. I worked hard, met new friends and began to establish myself as one to be watched. However, things were about to change. That night as I headed across the lobby to the cola machines, I passed most of the campers and counselors huddled around the television to watch the baseball all-star game.

Not interested in the game, I walked away minding my own business, and headed directly to the vending machines. One of the counselors (Kent) yelled out, "Hey, Kidder! Get over here. I need a back rub."

Having already been warned that the counselors often treated the kids as their personal lackies, I was ready. Besides, he already had two campers attending to his needs. Without further thought, I proclaimed, "I didn't come here to rub your back. I came to play basketball." I continued on my way.

Now that the entire camp was watching, he couldn't let it ride. He jumped to his feet and got right in my face and said, "What did you say?"

A little intimidated by his towering height and large biceps, I meekly repeated, "I'm here to play ball, not rub your back." He said, "We'll see about that," as he grabbed my arm.

Just then, a strange resolve came over me. I yanked my arm away and said, "Yes, we will see. I'm going to ask the coach if I have to rub your back." Kent consented, and I quickly headed down the hallway toward the coach's office while the campers quieted, waiting to see how this might end.

I knocked on the coach's door, and he quickly invited me in. To my surprise, he had apparently just gotten out of the shower. He sported

LA4 – Bonus

a t-shirt and sweatpants and was toweling off his hair while talking on the phone. I tried to exit quickly, but he encouraged me to tell him what the trouble seemed to be. I gave him the synopsis, and his answer was startling to say the least: "Tell him to Jack an eye!"

"What?"

He reiterated, "You don't have to rub his back. Tell him to Jack an eye."

"Thank you, Coach," I squeaked out on my way back to the boys. I was about to use a phrase that I'd heard neither before nor since. It sure sounded provocative, maybe even a little vulgar. I couldn't wait to use it.

As I entered the lobby, everyone was waiting for the verdict. With each step my confidence grew and grew. Finally, without missing a beat I looked the counselor in the eyes and blurted out: "Jack an eye."

Chins hit the floor and Kent jumped up and literally ran to cut me off. So I repeated myself, "The coach told me to tell you to 'Jack an eye.' Go ask him," I added. Then I walked out of the lobby, leaving a rather stunned group of campers and counselors behind.

Needless to say, the rest of my camp experience was tension filled. The counselors who refereed our games let people foul me without a call and in turn, called fouls on me I never committed. The other kids stayed clear of me for obvious reasons, and at 15, this was tough to take emotionally.

Admittedly, I went to bed a couple of nights with a few tears in my eyes, but somehow managed to turn in the best performance of my basketball life as I led my team in scoring and to the championship. I also made it to the finals in two individual competitions. But to nobody's surprise, my name did not appear on the all-star roster.

Sadly, what should have been at least a moment of joy and accomplishment for a young boy ended only in a burning sense of injustice. I'm willing to bet that you too have a few of those lodged in your gut as well — a moment of triumph ruined by poor leadership or abuse of power.

But before we curse everyone that ever hurt us, let's make that burn count. Let's make a decree that we will not abuse our power, our realm of authority. Every day we have an opportunity to knock someone down or build them up. So when things get tough, let's forget about the "Jack an Eye," an "Eye for an Eye," and remember, "The greatest of these is love."

HARASSMENT CYBER STYLE

> **LA4** *TERM*
> A cyber bully, like the bully defined in the previous section, feels the need to hurt others to make himself feel good, significant or even powerful. The cyber bully is even a bigger coward hiding behind the platform known as social media.

Harassment from a cyber bully should be even easier to overcome because his only power is the written word. He is not with you to speak those words to your ears or hurt you physically in any way. Ironically, and unfortunately, in today's world, the cyber bully can become even more powerful than a human being you see every day: we'll discuss that a little later on.

LESSON 1

Quick thought

Before I begin to expose the many problems that have manifested in our society from social media for both the young and the old alike, let's first acknowledge the positive opportunities the internet has to offer: we can research schools for our children, explore restaurants, businesses and shopping malls. We can access information from all over the globe at a push of a button, allowing us to see and understand other nations and people like never before. And on a personal level, we can enjoy our friends and family from afar.

LA4 - Bonus

However, for many the "cyber life" becomes more important than reality. Folks of all ages invest their time, emotions and personal image letting their lives play out on the likes of Facebook, Twitter and Instagram unknowingly empowering a cyber bully to invade and crash that imaginary world anytime he wants. There are already several studies to suggest that those who spend an exorbitant amount of time on social media struggle with anxiety, depression and other psychological issues.

There's an old proverb that says, "Hang out at your neighbor's house too long and he will learn to hate you." I say hang out in the same place too long, and you'll get a well-deserved punch in the nose. Even if it's not a literal punch, it will feel like it. And trust me, in the long term, you'll be thankful for it. Please read this true story of something that happened to me when I was younger, and you'll understand what I mean.

Storytime

"The Summer of Regret … And the Fist I Met"

Discussion questions

Why do you suppose that I kept going back to Greg's house even though I knew it was no good and it was getting old?

_____
_____
_____
_____
_____

Have you been in a similar situation where you kept returning to something, someone or somewhere even though you knew it was not good for you or even that enjoyable anymore? What would you do differently now if you had the chance?

_____
_____
_____

Bonus Section

How did it make you feel when I called Ricky and exposed his lies? Can you see the parallel between Ricky's made-up life and the made-up lives that people project on the internet?

Did that dose of reality feel refreshing?

Have you ever had your false reality exposed? Have you ever exposed somebody else? Were things better after the truth was known?

> "Hang out in the same place too long and you will get a well-deserved punch in the nose. Even if it's not a literal punch, it will feel like it. And trust me, in the long term, you'll be thankful for it."

LA4 - Bonus

LESSON 2

Quick Thought

Most of these two lessons on Cyber Bullying deal with you and how you can be successful in life as well as overcome harassment. However, please remember, like with all bullies, cyber bullies need to be exposed. Don't assume that just because the accusing, lying or making threats is on the internet, that everyone knows—including all authority figures. Tell your friends. Contact your superiors and even the police if the situation is that extreme. Don't let these cowards get away with anything, whether they are talking about you or somebody else. Shine the light, baby!

And finally, please remember the entire purpose of LA4—to improve in honor and integrity. When you're working at that on a daily basis, what can anybody say negatively about you? I know: Nobody's perfect. But when you're working to honor and improve your integrity, everybody will know. It's obvious. And ultimately bullies of all kinds will stop the harassment and stay away from you because your courage exposes their nonsense.

Storytime

"Ode to the Party Line"

Discussion questions

Have you ever had a moment of truth where it was time to "grow up" and move on? What was it?

_____
_____
_____
_____
_____
_____
_____

Have you said things and/or posted things online that would have been better left unsaid? Were there repercussions?

_____
_____
_____
_____
_____
_____

Have you taken an honest look at your own "cyber life" to see if it might be out of balance? What measures will you take to pull it back into balance and make sure that does not happen again?

_____
_____
_____
_____
_____
_____

Life Applications

All of this discussion of cyber bullying and cyber life still hits on the heart of the issue: Honor and Integrity, making sure we are careful what we say or write about others and that we do not tolerate harassment/bullies in any form. We need to expose them. And remember this: there is one word that separates the successful from the unsuccessful, the truth tellers from the liars and if you like, the godly from the ungodly. That word is discipline. And it's something that takes a force of focus and attention every single day. That is the courageous life and the life worth living.

LA4 – Bonus

Summer of Regret and the Fist I Met

I remember well the summer I was 13 years old. Even though that was 30 years ago, I remember it because I did nothing—nothing useful anyway. The thought of that wasted time still haunts me, motivates me to never forget the preciousness of a single day, especially a summer day.

It was the last summer of my life that I would not be required to have a steady job, and I spent it sitting around Greg Juday's house. Greg lived in town just a short bike ride from my country home and although he was a year younger than I, we got along okay. The draw to spend time with Greg was not so much a buddy-buddy relationship; it had more to do with the fact that his parents were not home during the day. I guess there was sort of a freedom there, yet every day when I left I felt like a part of me was dying.

It's not that we did anything wrong anyway. We watched TV, sat around inside and out and sometimes ran around the house. It was pointless. Interestingly enough, there was but one major event that did take place there right before summer would end and launch us into a new grade in school. This event would cure me of the Greg Juday blues forever.

Greg and I were sitting on the porch killing time, per usual, one afternoon when Mike, a younger and much rougher character, came walking toward Greg's house. I didn't think much of it at first since Mike dropped by from time to time to share a few new cuss words or phrases he had learned from his even shadier older brother. Only this time, somebody was following Mike—somebody gigantic whom we'd never seen before.

He and Mike made themselves at home on Greg's porch. We were told that "Ricky" was Mike's 15-year-old cousin from the city. He was from a much larger town; he was much larger, and he told tales that were larger yet.

For the next few days Mike and Ricky seemed to stop by Greg's porch more and more with exaggerated stories of Ricky's greatness. We were told that Ricky was a Karate black belt as well as a dirt bike champion and the yarn did spin and spin.

Finally, I could take it no more. Greg and I got on the phone one afternoon and called up Mike's house and asked for Ricky. When he answered, all I wanted to say for days just poured out: "Hey Ricky, I'd sure like to see those trophies, Vrrrm Vrrrm! You couldn't stay on a bike let-alone race one. You big-fat liar!" And the insults kept coming until I finally hung up as Greg and I laughed uncontrollably. That was the most fun I had there all summer until we looked across the street and saw Ricky and Mike coming in a huff.

Greg quickly locked the door in the kitchen and we continued to laugh as the two boys approached. I couldn't resist from tossing a few more insults as Ricky glared at me through the screen door.

Ricky pounded the door a few times and then made a threat to Greg, "You better open this door before I break it down."

I just chuckled all the more until Greg walked directly over and unlooked the door. To this day, I have no idea what he was thinking. I froze with my mouth wide open. Finally, I came to my senses, but it was too late—there was no where to run. I just walked into the dining room with Ricky right on my heels. He didn't say anything. He just handed his cigarette to Mike, stepped up to me and punched me in the face four or five times.

He retrieved his cigarette and calmly walked out of the house. I stood there in shock for a moment, then ran to my bike and peddled away never to return to Greg's house again.

I went home but told nobody what had just happened. It was like a dream. I could see him hitting my face, but I didn't feel anything, well, at least until the next morning. But I didn't care. I was alive again. I had been knocked right out of that stupor I had been in most of the summer.

And I wasn't sorry. I wasn't sorry it happened, and I wasn't sorry for what I had said to Ricky. It was the truth. And the only regret I had was that this didn't happen in the first few weeks of summer instead of the last.

It's funny. The pain from those punches lasted but a few days, but the bitterness from those wasted summer days still sits in a corner in my soul. And I'm glad because never again do I want to take for granted the summer sun, imagination or youth.

Ode to the Party Line

When I was 10 years old, my family and I lived in a small suburban neighborhood. The houses looked much the same: small ranch style homes with evenly cut lawns. By 1970's standards, we were neither rich nor poor.

However, you would think that we could have afforded our own telephone line. It must have saved my father all of $3 per month to be on the "Party Line" as opposed to a private line.

(For those who never had the privilege, a Party Line is just that: three or four other homes sharing the same line. You may pick up the phone and hear a dial tone at one point and a few moments later try to dial out again and instead of the dial tone, you would hear one of your fellow partiers engrossed in their own conversation.) I know, how inconvenient! Right? Well, for adults maybe, but for a young boy and his nine-year-old companion, this offered a standby activity when summer outdoor festivities got a little tiresome.

We pulled the same stunts (that's an adult word for an annoying child's antics) nearly every day. First, my buddy Mikey and I shared the receiver. We stood ear-to-ear so we could both hear and it wasn't long before heavy breathing or rude comments, for example, "is that so", began to pour out of our mouths. Immediately, we were greeted with the same daily response: "You kids cut that out. I've had just about enough." The more frustrated the tone, the more we liked it.

We also enjoyed the occasional clicking of the ringer. I actually learned this one from my mother who had waited over an hour one day just to call my dad at work. I guess she figured that was long enough and sent her own message. If there's one thing kids enjoy, it's watching adults get crabby with one another.

Interestingly enough, Mikey and I were not limited just to our party line pals. We also knew what to do when we got a dial tone: get out the phonebook, pick a name that made us laugh and make "crank" calls. We only knew one: "Is your refrigerator running? You better go catch it!"

You would think after all the practice we had, our timing would be flawless, but Mikey got nervous every time it was his turn. He would either say the punch line too soon and too fast, or he would forget it altogether.

Can you image working around the house one afternoon when the phone rings and on the other side you hear a little boy's voice proclaim quickly, "Is your refrigerator running?" CLICK.

And no matter how badly Mikey performed, his response was always the same. He hopped around our kitchen on both feet excitingly all the while chanting, "How was that? How was that?" Hey, I was his buddy. What could I say? "Nice job!"

Caller ID has pretty much put a stop to this little number; however, there seems to be a new way of phone entertainment these days: "Smart" phones - phone antics for adults. People talk when they've nothing to say and say things that are left better unsaid and show photos that reflect an imaginary world that only exists online.

At least Mikey and I had an excuse; we were ornery little boys with nothing to do. But by the time we hit 10 or 11 years old, we grew out of it. Is your smart phone running? Maybe you should let it go.

Troy

LA4 – Bonus

NOTES

www.ingramcontent.com/pod-product-compliance
Lightning Source LLC
Chambersburg PA
CBHW061123070526
44583CB00028B/3367